THE I
SNAKE

PEACE TEAM FORWARD

A METHODOLOGY OF PEACE, NOT WAR

A VIEW OF THE PAST
AND A PLAN FOR THE FUTURE

Harry Wagner
Edited by Renee Darby

Copyright © 2018 by Harry Wagner/Peace Team Forward.

All rights reserved. No part of this publication may be reproduced, distributed or transmitted in any form or by any means, including photocopying, record-ing, or other electronic or mechanical methods, without the prior written per-mission of the publisher, except in the case of brief quotations embodied in critical reviews and certain other noncommercial uses permitted by copyright law. For permission requests, write to the publisher, addressed "Attention: Permissions Coordinator," at the address below.

Harry Wagner/Peace Team Forward
1061 Boones Bridge Rd
Madison, GA 30650

Book Layout ©2018 BookDesignTemplates.com

Ordering Information:

Quantity sales. Special discounts are available on quantity purchases by cor-porations, associations, and others. For details, contact the "Special Sales De-partment" at the address above.

The Headless Snake/ Harry Wagner. —1st ed.
ISBN 978-1-9877924-1-6

Contents

PREFACE 5
INTRODUCTION 9
CHAPTER 1 MILITARY 21
CHAPTER 2 PERSUASION WITH RELEVANCE 45
CHAPTER 3 PEACE TEAM FORWARD 93
CHAPTER 4 TRANSITION 111
CHAPTER 5 PHOENIX-ICEX 127
CHAPTER 6 CHIEU HOI 147
CHAPTER 7 TORTURE 171
CHAPTER 8 EVENTS 193
CHAPTER 9 CREDENTIALS 233
CHAPTER 10 PHOTOS 245
EPILOGUE 253

GLOSSARY OF ACRONYMS AND ABBREVIATIONS 257

PREFACE

The failures of military leadership to address and correct their internal problems and the loss of Congressional integrity has put the security of this nation at risk.

Peace Team Forward is a beginning. An advocacy for a moral conscience and foreign policy with integrity.

It is now time to start to rebuild, replace, and start anew.

I am talking about the Executive branch of our government, especially, the Departments of Defense, State, and Treasury.

I started research for this book 10 years ago because what I was reading and hearing of my government was contrary to what it once was 62 years ago, the year I reported for service at Fort Bragg, NC, 82nd ABN Division, 44th Tank Battalion, 1st Lt, jumpmaster, cryptographer clearances. Now at 87 years of age, loaded with experiences including 22 months in Vietnam as assigned General Officer 1966-1968, I have taken the time to research what is wrong with America and increasingly getting worse with our government. By August

25, 2013, I thought I had finished writing this book; then President Obama mouthed off on Syria. It proved my point. It is now January 12, 2018.

Since 9/11 and the Bush years when the government declared war against terrorism and the President took charge of the American military, the military has accomplished little you could claim as successful. The military has left a trail of unsuccessful deployments and thousands of non-combatant deaths and injured, with whole countries in ruin with stark memories of the atrocities committed against their civilian population. My Vietnam experience was at the essential point in time that the military, in an effort to salvage a victory, began converting from conventional war to a counterinsurgency strategy that failed. And that advanced the Phoenix Program, often referred to as "murder incorporated" as the final solution directed by one William Colby, CIA. I was assigned to the Phoenix Saigon staff while working from the Embassy to develop Psychological Operations for the Program.

1967-1968, the two most combative years for the American military, I was a member of the IFFV General Staff working with combat units on psycho-logical operations in the field and Chieu Hoi. The Vietnam War was five times larger in commitment of troops than the Iraq and Afghan deployments.

My first encounter with this new program was a briefing; "Cut the head off the snake and the snake dies; if we eliminate the enemy leadership, it will fail." You will find in this book why the exact opposite was true. And why the military continues to fail at warfare for several reasons, even after many attempts of post-Vietnam rebuilding and what appeared to be a program of musical chairs played by Generals. You will find the singularly most obvious reason has been in front of them the whole time. The military lacks leadership; it is so blinded by tradition. As long as they keep seeing themselves from only one side of the mirror, in today's and future deployments, results will be problematical.

The primary reason for this book is to establish means to reduce or eliminate unnecessary violence that comes with war strategies in use today by our military that has created millions of civilian deaths. The era of main force battles on land is over; the advances in military technology of weapons and missiles have fostered the development of ground forces comprised of small, specialized units. These specialized units bring with them the problem of control and coordination of their deployment; they tend to operate in secrecy, as necessary due to their size and management. They can become political and economic problems. And whatever you call them, they are military invaders.

In the search for non-violent methods in developing the means to attract and sustain the support of the indigenous population, we developed and tested the *Persuasion with Relevance* strategy in 30 different missions within unsecured territory of South Vietnam. We developed intelligence gathering methods without EIT (enhanced interrogation techniques), many times more productive than the use of torture or the customary methods of interrogation.

Supporting data for this book is in my possession, my reports, briefing papers, and mission assignments, original documents shipped from Saigon to the States. This book is not either censored or edited by the government. It contains no currently classified information. It is critical of and suggests improvements of, the military as to the transformation to a better military.

This is not in any way a hint for disarmament, but a lead toward a more civilized and successful utilization of our military. It is unbelievable that of all the restructuring and transforming that has been applied to our military since Vietnam, the schooling and "Think Tank" studies and analyses have failed to produce a realistic management leadership program. We must stop the further decline of the United States of America's position as realistic world leadership and cease the erosion of our Constitutional freedoms and establish peaceful associations.

The military is suffering from lack of enough good line officers and senior NCO's. They need leadership training, a comprehensive policy, and training of personnel of all ranks. Rewriting traditional policies and renaming them just doesn't work in a world that has, and is continuing, to advance from benefits of technology as fast as the United States of America. If the military will transition into a new concept, it can lead the world into a new and better humanity. The military's track record of successful deployments since Vietnam (1972) is not only embarrassing but disgusting. I seek to help change it; America is my country.

Letter from the author:

Most of this writing is based on personal experience; much of it is from the opportunities I happened to be at, the right place at the right time. Some of these were unique in location and circumstances.

As a beginning statement, I want to emphasize a point to make sure it is understood. To all those who have and those who are currently serving in the American Armed Forces, you have my eternal gratitude and respect for your duty to country. In this writing, I am very critical of methods that have been deployed to include tactics and strategy that have been used to the detriment of many lives and property. My criticism is aimed at those in the Department of Defense, Congress, and White House who have grossly abused the use of our military power, for whatever objective they had in mind.

You will find in my bio-data reasons and events that influenced my life. There is one very early memory from childhood. This was before TV and FM radio; days of "Jack Armstrong the All-American Boy", "The Shadow", "I love a Mystery", "The Inner Sanctum", "Don Winslow of the Navy", etc.

There was one radio show I remember and it has always been in my mind; it was a radio play about the life of a young boy. The story explored his successes in later life and that he would discover the cure for cancer, but he was killed at age ten by a drunk driver. The point this story drilled into my mind- no life is expendable, all have potential and purpose to an unknown degree; only life lived can expose the true value of a life.

To have experienced the tragedy of modern warfare with the knowledge that hundreds, even thousands, of non-combatant civilian populations are murdered almost daily, and some were American military efforts to grasp military dominance over foreign people, is unconscionable. We can debate the reasons for these attacks but the methods utilized are not; they are heinous, murderous, uncivilized. I saw enough that it damaged my perception of humanity. The purpose of this writing is to inform you, the reader, that this type warfare is unnecessary and is always counterproductive; *there is a proven strategy that produces a much more favorable and productive result...***PERSUASION WITH RELEVANCE**

INTRODUCTION

TO SAIGON, VIETNAM FROM FRIENDSWOOD, TEXAS

As you will soon notice I am not a professional writer, what is written in this book is what I saw and what I did in Vietnam. As Sargent Friday once said; "The facts, ma'am, just the facts." This book is about the military, about the facts and not interviews or legends arising from the telling of combat. There are as reported 3,000 books about Vietnam, most relate to the conduct of war and the carnage that was created. This book is based on extensive re-search and on my experience in Vietnam dealing with the traditional military and the need for a different military approach as an operational strategy for these "small or irregular wars." It is not a book just about Vietnam. It is a book of how the Vietnam War influenced our military and government with the Headless Snake concept of the Phoenix Program.

I began to assemble all of my files brought from Vietnam 1966-1968, and years of research of recent CIA-Military deployments; it became clear that there were several different subjects that should each be described individu-ally, and yet they were all interrelated to the Vietnam War and the results of that war. The Vietnam War is still connected to the present day American military, and the Phoenix Program became the keystone of today's founda-tion for our military. Vietnam after 1968 became a disaster, and the idea that the Phoenix Program with the murders it promoted (and that's what they were) could turn the battle into an American victory was based on the conceit of the CIA and one William Colby. What I have assembled here is my viewpoint as seen by me, a participant, not a careerist bureaucrat, or an Academy grad-uate, or politician So, you will find how I organized the telling of my experi-ence in an index of the major subjects, operations, and missions in Vietnam. I was responsible as a Program Director and Advisor on the General Staff of

IFFV in Region II and among other things assigned special assignments out of the Embassy for the White House. Copies of my credentials and my assignments are included in this book.

You should understand that my experiences as related are not the result of interviews but actual on-the-ground experiences. These experiences with my security clearances granted me access to many high-level intelligence briefings and reports of MACV, CIA-Military, and Vietnamese, plus almost unlimited travel in the country via military and Air America.

This is not a book central to the carnage of war, but about people caught up in an unnecessary war as viewed by a non-career contract employee to the Department of State, USAID.

My writing is both critical and constructive, produced freely without command oversight or career centered restrictions, or fear of censorship. The world has been and will continue to be a violent place, created by men who believe aggression and dominance are essential elements of government because they have been so trained and lack a true understanding of the universal rights of all men. Traditional military is still failing to accomplish logical objectives; recent changes as of yet have failed to make the necessary modifications that are still in front of them every day. A major realignment is long past due…renaming things or producing another 200-page instruction manual is not a sufficient adjustment. War is war, with guns and uniforms, with all the other military trappings they display.

I am not now or for the last 44 years been a government employee; I claim no credits as an academician. I have served my country when called, as you will see in my credentials and how I relate my opinion of the failed leadership and conduct of the war. To emphasize the tragedies of the war serves no purpose at this time, but the failure in purpose, leadership, and conduct of the war does.

I do not apologize for my conduct with USAID supervisors; some were ex-perienced and very capable, while others were inexperienced and capable of creating problems that were producing unnecessary risks to life. I was never assigned to the position I was employed, as a Senior Provincial Advisor for

USAID. Instead, I was assigned to the Vietnamese Psychological Operations program Chieu Hoi; it interfaced with all intelligence groups and military units.

The reader must make adjustments as to the source of many of the books written about Vietnam, mostly centered about the way the American military managed the war and the terribly savage attacks made against the civilian populations. Remember that up to 680,000 American military were involved plus another 500,000 South Vietnamese and other allied military. It was a long war, and up until 1969 it had been managed and fought developing methods thought to be capable enough to defeat the VC and NVA. However, the February 1968 Tet major offensive by the enemy put everything in doubt.

I was recruited by USAID from being mayor of Friendswood, Texas to being Senior Provincial Advisor in Vietnam. It was later that I learned their recruiting drive for personnel to send to Vietnam was fading out with limited results, and they did not discover in their push to recruit me that I was not the profile of a typical government employee. They took me for good or bad. I was a true "generalist" and at 37 years of age experienced with a lot of "street knowledge," with military (82nd ABN Division, Jump Master, Armor Officer), aerospace manufacturing methods engineer, municipal judge, and mayor of a small, rapidly growing city outside Houston, Texas, near NASA in Galveston County, and career as being mostly self-employed.

I arrived with not a minute of training or orientation about the mission which gave me an advantage; having not been officially learned, I was to learn at the source by experience and common sense in a war at the time we had difficulty adjusting our strategy in hope of defeating the VC/NVA, a "guerilla army."

I arrived in 1966 and departed 22 months later. You will read how this American, brought up as nonmilitary with little political background, got the job done with integrity, reacted to the overly bureaucratic government disaster, the Vietnam War.

The experience of being in a Senior position afforded me the opportunity to work at everything I was not hired to do; I was contracted by USAID to be a Senior Provincial Advisor to one of the Vietnamese 44 provinces. Due to the incompetence of USAID getting my papers to Vietnam in a timely manner, I was assigned to a quasi-military position as a Regional Chieu Hoi Advisor in IFFV-II Corps and IFFV Military General Staff in charge of Psychological Operations with added special assignments from the Embassy and CIA. In many respects, it was the best introduction to Vietnam, the Vietnamese, and the war.

My authority in Vietnam came as a matter of my ability and resulting from the coincidence of circumstance and time. My view of Vietnam was from briefing the Generals down to the Privates in the field, from Embassy meetings to airmobile assaults in the field. My anonymity was necessary to successfully operate in the field undisturbed by USAID and military careerists; this gave me additional freedom to make contacts with the right people, both American and Vietnamese (government, VC, and NVA). I was never restricted in gaining access to any information, data, or equipment I required for my Chieu Hoi and Psychological Operations, ICEX- Phoenix, or Special Assignments. My authority was never to be questioned in the field by any military unit or command. The Embassy assignments ranged from refugee problems to assassinations.

The resulting authority enabled me to move freely and control things, do things because I got jobs done, and work across the various organizations as MACV, CIA, USAID, Special Forces, ROK, and Vietnamese government organizations. The Chieu Hoi Program was involved in every aspect of the war, giving me contacts with American and Vietnamese country-wide. My initial rank was FSRO 3/1, but as the mission was being reorganized and assembled as CORDS, it was raised to 3/3. CORDS combined all military and civilian personnel under one central command. All civilians were required to sign an agreement to comply with the military UCMJ (Uniform Code of Military Justice) or be terminated from contract without prejudice. I became a General Staff member of IFFV (First Field Forces Vietnam) whereas Chief of Chieu Hoi I dealt with all military units with their psychological operations (utilizing persuasion rather than threats). As the staff officer of IFFV, I was knowledgeable of all II Corps military activities; I had oversight responsibility for all psychological missions for IFFV and assisted in military intelligence. The Chieu Hoi defectors provided unlimited intelligence if you knew how to get it, which was one of my primary interests, how to influence the VC/NVA into defecting to the government.

Results further elevated my authority by accomplishments and being able to work in the field with other programs and personnel. I gave all the credit for the success of Region II Chieu Hoi to the Vietnamese we worked with. Psy-chological Operations gave much-needed support to the army psy-ops units and helped these units that had little leverage to promote programs within the combat divisions. My presence on the General Staff IFFV created the au-thority to be accepted by senior officers in the various combat units, and to obtain better methods and intelligence for development of psycho-logical products for use in support of the military field operations My pres-ence in control of psy-ops gave the units leverage they had not had before.

The access to the top military commanders from the four regions at the Commanders Conferences as a briefer also allowed me to listen to all of the other military briefers. These briefings were attended by a small group of the most senior officers. In most military briefings, there was always a request for conditions of the Chieu Hoi Program as a priority program.

This book is my way of "coming clean," to expose what I believe as an American; the massive misuse of our military power and military personnel as it is now deployed around the world. My first priority is to present a strategy, Persuasion with Relevance, to reduce the loss of lives, especially non-combatants; as a strategy it was field tested and successful against the Viet Cong, North Vietnamese Military, and Chinese (PLA) Military Advisors deployed in South Vietnam.

There will be statements herein based on my personal experiences that are seriously critical of the military. I make no apology for this; it is not against the individuals serving in our military because I honor their service standing between us and harm. I am eternally grateful for their service and sacrifice, each and every one.

Vietnam brought to light the idea that large-scale military strategies were impracticable, if not unpopular, but the irregular wars and counterinsurgency wars could be justified by using Hunter-Killer tactics and surges that have been pretty much kept out of the news. But there was a problem in the need for better intelligence to identify the indigenous enemy leaders and their locations at various times. Following the concept "if you cut the head off the snake, it dies;" that is true with snakes, but with popular uprisings and insurgencies the opposite is true. Enemy leaders are just that, leaders; the killers are invaders and such logic as killing the leadership is counter-productive toward reaching any sort of settlement between the opposing parties. And too often the collateral killing of civilians further complicates reaching any agreements.

The success of this type of aggressive tactics depends upon good intelligence, which is not easily obtained in these irregular type wars. To enhance intelligence gathering they have employed torture with no methods barred from use on suspects or prisoners. These heinous crimes on humanity have been supported by the highest government officials. Once this starts, it is impossible to stop, and as it continues it is the indicator that methods have failed in the initial efforts to control the situation. The last effort to follow torture is the total destruction of the enemy, that being all of their indigenous population and property. It is warfare without conscious respect for human life.

I am opposed to these measures because they have never been successful and create generations of hate. I recognize that in circumstances where violence cannot be avoided it must be overcome before any thought of nega-tions can be considered. The military response must be measured to the point that it does not make the situation worse for the indigenous population.

The requirement to influence indigenous populations in past wars produced programs such as pacification, military civic action, and winning hearts and minds; these actually had limited success. But today with real -

time worldwide communications of news, both voice and visual programming with applied psychological coercion influencing the public opinion of the world, the damage done by the superior military force can be counterproduc-tive. These visual reports of collateral deaths and destruction of property make winning hearts and minds very difficult, usually impossible to excuse.

Our field operations to develop the best way to deal with the population was to be non-military in appearance and organized as possible but show strength of purpose and ask one simple question, "How can I earn your trust?" Let them lead the recovery; this way you will find field intelligence and secu-rity will also improve. Avoid the appearance and actions of a dominant force; show strength by your cooperation and positive support of their recovery. The last issue to determine is the number of months the Team must stay on the job; frequent rotation of personnel weakens the cooperation of the pop-ulation. Birthdays, weddings, deaths, and holidays are memories, when shared they make good friends.

If the United States of America is ever to recover a position as world leader it will never, by the nature of man, do it with its military deployed on foreign land claiming rights of aggression by false unproven acts.

Leave the military at home to defend the country; deploy our assistance only when requested. Instead of invading and destroying property and killing to take control of resources and key transport right of ways, we should be nation building, working with and not against. Our military leadership must take note that our two-ocean defense is the past; now in the age of technology, it offers no security. The military aggressive overseas deploy-ments have in fact destroyed our homeland security. There appears no other rational as to why, other than greed and the incompetence of our leadership.

It is time to take stock of our condition, our respect for life, our one-time ability to lead, and work *among* the sovereign countries rather than *over* them. Think what our efforts with thousands of Americans dead and wounded; billions of dollars wasted and again failing to leave with "A job well done, America;" we are just lucky to withdraw, period. Rethink how those lives and billions of dollars could have been utilized to build, rather than destroy and kill.

Our leadership must realign itself because one more of these costly, ill-advised adventures and the world will collectively demand compensations which we cannot pay due to the mismanagement of our financial and industrial wealth that has been wasted by the military. The required transition of the military is the basis for this book. My opinion is the result of the unusually wide range of military assignments, which many times was given not to be questioned as to the authority from my contacts at the Embassy to get results, both in civilian and military matters. I was cleared to use my judgment to get the requested results. My writing is based on my experience in Vietnam and not on interviews of those there 45 years ago. My senior rank (General) and high military security clearances gave me immediate access to many classified reports, briefings, and meetings at the highest levels of military command.

No, I don't infer we give up our military; I believe we must keep it strong and technically advanced as possible, to speak softly but carry a big stick. We will advance this nation further into the future if we deploy Peace Team Forward, which could be developed as the Shield with the Spear Team. I had the opportunity to participate several times in US Military "Sweep and Search" operations and compared them to Persuasion with Relevance. If you couldn't see the difference, you could feel it from the people.

The need to make changes in our military alignment is obvious. This book is my honest effort to explain some of history and the incentive to promote the fact things can be different and made much more productive for the United States of America.

THE HARRY WAGNER FAMILY HAS A LONG JOURNEY AHEAD—STORY ON PAGE 2. Lisa Points Out Goal to Mark and David (Sitting on the Floor); Brother Matt Looks On

Pearland Friendswood Personals

Harry W. Wagner received an armload of psuedo-Oriental gifts and an earful of jokes about sewer plant enzymes and dances at the City Hall Saturday evening when about 50 friends entertained the former Friendswood mayor and his wife at a farewell party. Wagner is leaving soon for a State Department assignment in Viet Nam.

"The real reason I'm going to Viet Nam," Wagner joked in the spirit of the occasion, "is that I'm determined to make Pol-Con work somewhere." Pol-Con is the trade name of the experimental sewer plant enzyme which created considerable controversy in Friendswood during the last months of his administration.

Mrs. Clay Hicks was in charge of arrangements for the dinner. L.D. Thorn was master of ceremonies, and John Moore gave a humorous talk. Dr. Barney Myatt gave the invocation.

HARRY WAGNER IN COOLIE COAT, HAT
Mrs. Wagner Laughs at the Farewell Gifts

Town of Friendswood says goodbye to former mayor and family.

Ex-Friendswood Mayor
Wagner Going To Work For U.S. in Viet Nam

Harry D. Wagner, who served a stormy two-year term as mayor of Friendswood, is going to South Viet Nam to fight bigger political battles as an official of the U.S. Department of State.

He has been appointed a provincial representative attached to the United States Operations Mission of the Agency for International Development.

Wagner will go to Washington for a briefing on Aug. 29. Then he and his family will board a plane for Manila, P.I., where he will have two weeks to help wife Barbara and the four children get settled in a new home before he reports to Saigon.

"I don't know whether I'll be assigned to a city or to a foxhole," he said, "but I know it will be a challenging assignment. I'm looking forward to a new career with the State Department."

Wagner's new job will be part of the AID's "counter-insurgency" program, designed to promote anti-Communist political, social and psychological development in South Viet Nam. The program has been called "the other war" in Viet Nam, and Wagner anticipates that his job will continue and expand when the shooting war is over.

As provincial representative in one of the country's 44 provinces, or states, he and an American military adviser will work directly with the Vietnamese provincial governor.

In part, the nature of his work will be determined by the sector to which he is assigned. In some areas the provincial representatives are involved almost entirely with military operations, refugee relief, and medical assistance. In others there is a substantial amount of "self-help" already in progress, involving agriculture, education, health and small public works projects.

His State Department job description outlines a three-phase plan for rural rehabilitation which includes clear-

> See Pear-i-scope for information on Harry Wagner's offer to say "hello" to relatives of Progress readers in Viet Nam.

ing the areas, securing them, and building.

"In clearing," says the job description form, "military forces sweep the Viet Cong armed units from a designated area. In the securing phase, friendly military and paramilitary forces stay in place and hold the area while civil government control and services are installed and local self-defense forces organized... In the building phase, increasing emphasis is placed on creating effective and just local government and on economic and social improvement...so that the strength and determination of the people to resist either the subversive or military re-entry of the Viet Cong will continue, and so that the regular military forces may be completely withdrawn for undertaking clearing operations in other areas."

The job is not without hazards. One AID representative, Joseph W. Grainger, has been killed by enemy fire, and another, Gustav Hertz, is a prisoner of the Viet Cong.

No dependents of U.S. military or civilian personnel have been allowed in Viet Nam since last February. However, in Wagner's job classification a $300 per

Continued on Page 3

Wagner Sees Need To Help Viet Nam

Continued from Page 2

month allowance will be made for his family's housing in Manila. He will have an opportunity to visit them at government expense two or three times a year.

Counting the family living allowance and extra pay for working in a hazardous area, Wagner said his new position would be "about a $30,000-a-year job."

Wagner has long been a believer in person-to-person communications to overcome international misunderstandings.

While he was mayor of Friendswood he tried to find a way to bring two Vietnamese high school students to live in Friendswood for a year, but he was unable to make the arrangements.

Such a project was still on his mind recently when he saw a State Department ad in the Houston newspapers offering various types of employment in the war zone.

He made an appointment for an interview, "mostly out of curiosity," he said, and learned that he qualified for the provincial representative post.

His term as mayor of Friendswood was one of the deciding factors, he was told. Wagner is 36 years old, and he was one of the youngest mayors in the nation while he was in office. He was defeated in a bid for re-election last April.

Another qualification which impressed the interviewers was his military experience as an officer and jump master with a paratroop unit. His work with Boy Scouts and his college degrees in business and engineering also were taken into consideration.

Wagner is a partner in Steel and Machine Tool Sales, Inc. and he is qualified to design and produce metal products and to do computer programming for machine tools.

"I have a good many avocations, and now they're paying off," he said.

Wagner said he believes the United States has an obligation to be in Viet Nam and that "if we are to fight Communism in another country we must provide foreign aid for rehabilitation.

"I don't want to sound like a missionary, but I do feel that I have volunteered for a mission."

If he is a missionary in a sense, Wagner will come close to fulfilling the prediction his mother made when he was a boy in Portsmouth, Ohio. The family was active in the Presbyterian church, and she expected young Harry to become a minister.

Wagner and his wife, who is a native of Canton, Ohio, have been married for 12 years and have lived in Friendswood since 1962.

Mrs. Wagner has been the chief organizer and director of the Friendswood Branch of Rosenberg Library, which was opened in the new City Hall during her husband's term as mayor. She also has been active in P-TA, church, and other community activities.

The Wagners have four children, Matt, Mark, David and Lisa.

Friends of Mr. and Mrs. Wagner will honor them with a farewell dinner Saturday evening at King's Inn. About 120 guests have been invited.

CHAPTER 1

MILITARY

This book is based on field experience in Vietnam War and seemingly endless research on reports of America's pursuit of world dominance for control and profit for the few.

It has been 10 years since I started researching for this book and still, there are many questionable political, financial, military situations and events that I am not comfortable in my understanding of them. I seek solutions and offer alternatives as corrections.

As I was writing I tried to think of some way to make the purpose of this book perceptible to the reader as to the ends our government leadership has gone with the country's wealth and blood. Look at the Vietnam War; we gave up 58,148 American lives. If the average coffin is 7 feet in length that equals, if placed end to end, a total of 407,036 feet of flag-draped coffins. We can visualize this as 77 miles of Americans, lost for what? We lost that war and others since then; why? For security of the 50 states, I don't think so. For the "New World Order," yes, maybe. For the military-industrial complex prof-its and political power, **YES**.

True, my opinion is a product of my family life, education, and my path through 87 years of experiences. This book is a product of those years and highlights those things I am concerned about. I am not in a position to influence financial faults, only to know that the economic advantages that the cre-ation of our Constitutional government has provided have been compromised by the criminality of the bankers in control of our money and have depleted the wealth of the working Americans.

The greed of the elite corporations for control and profits have falsified world conditions with the war against terrorists to expand their control all over the world via our military and industrial complex. The military is over-sized and operating at the expense supported by taxing the American people with an accumulating debt that can never be paid. From recent review, the military has not balanced its books, but if correctly done would owe the American people trillions of dollars. The military and the government are the world's biggest racket. All of this adds up to a failed and corrupted central government with a future of greatly diminished prospects and to a substand-ard of living for many. The corruption has penetrated so completely that the electoral process will be more drama than reality, and until the corruption in our legislative is swept out and the lawmakers abide their duty to serve their country instead of themselves, it is another worthless taxpayer expense.

The analysis and understanding of current military problems from the data produced from research and my own past experience with the Vietnam War have led me to a decision that there is a combination of influences and failures. All of these must be addressed as intricate parts of the problem and made a part of any solution. They definitely require a transition of the military before they self-destruct from continued deployment failures. Mistakes in methods and conduct only make the pacification and civil action counter effective. Simply stated, our mistakes are forcing revenge prone populations forward into future generations for us to address, *somewhere, sometime*. This book includes my comments on policies, strategies, training, as well as lead-ership failure and failed strategy.

We can find fault in the military, and there is plenty wrong, but to focus on that without holding other systemic failures of government accountable is irresponsible, and if you have not noticed we have lost our place throughout

the world as the greatest nation. If our overseas missions a
acting to complex problems dealing with indigenous popul
change it.

War defies definition because there are always two or n
but always there is the defensive and the offensive viewpoin
has been a part of this nation from the "shot heard around the world" when the American farmers shot and killed two British soldiers at the Concord Bridge, the start of the American Revolution and the beginning of the end of heredity of ancestral titles as rulers. War is America's largest and most costly business; is it for freedom and liberty, or profits for the few? There is a better way for the USA to fit into the world of nations other than drones.

You will find descriptions of my activities in Vietnam, not as a storyline, but to illustrate a field tested and studied method of countering insurgencies and civil distressed populations Some of the illustrations of strategy are over-simplified as I used in the training of the indigenous population as active Team members. We learned from the people, as we say the "air we breathe," meaning close contact to integrate into their society. We found to go native was wrong but kept our presence as to who we were and why we were there. We were not recognized as military, which was the foremost feature of our presence. We came to assist them, to learn how to earn their trust.

Introducing a better deployment strategy that meets the Constitutional requirements and ideals of the American people, not just the military industrial complex of the elite corporations, is my goal. Our Declaration of Independence and articles of our Constitution establishes America as a humanitarian government. One would think that one of our first thoughts would be to sustain those features but actually, they have been totally ignored. If there is a problem anywhere in the world our military has an answer, a solution; and it will be a military one. Most likely, one of many they have promoted that failed, but renamed to try again without resolving why it failed.

Since then the government and military have labeled most of these occurrences as "conspiracies" or "terrorism," sounding less disturbing as calling what it is- "war." If a conspiracy does not happen frequently enough on its n, they have special operation teams over most of the world's governments. They can create one by following the National Security Strategy of the United States, which in simple terms is license to dominate the world by bringing all governments to a government of democracy. This is a declaration produced annually out of the White House, as the American government assumes they have a duty because they are the only world Super Power as a result of WWII. However, the experiences with unconventional warfare as in Vietnam, the lessons from it have been talked about a lot but ignored. Hitting on the insurgencies makes them stronger.

There have been estimates developed out of the carnage of war in the Middle East where we are fully engaged, that for every enemy military killed, six to eight civilians and some estimates as many as 28 to 1 are killed as collateral damage. Such losses to a society that is based on family structure create generations of hate and a source of enemy personnel. There are themes on this: "Sacrifice the few for the greater benefit of the many," "Killing the civilians because they are the necessary support of the fighters and should be eliminated." I assume these are applicable to any deployment as long it is them and not us as the "few" of the "World Super Power."

Our military could not defeat the Viet Cong in South Vietnam with the total control of the air and unlimited resources in support of their strategy and tactics. Then the 1968 Tet offensive by the VC/NVA revealed our weakness in strategy to defeat the North and our less than humane concern for civilians. We lost 58,000 KIA in the war and our ally lost several million. The CIA was given control of the war (they just took control) and from my observation, they operated independently from the military and failed to supply all of the critical intelligence they had to MACV. The control of the world's only Super Power was placed in William Colby as CORDS Director (the joint organization of all military and civilians in Vietnam) to direct the war's strategy.

Thus, Phoenix, the CIA's strategy to defeat the VC-NVA.

All of this bears on the decision to research and write this book, concentrating on our Military and the Department of Defense, a subject I have some experience with. My effort works to push for a transition of the military to cleanse itself before it too becomes a totally corrupted tool of the elite corporations and the New World Order. Both are self-centered and have no respect for the inalienable rights of all people, a position I cannot tolerate.

My primary interest is Psychological Operations, to create a consensus of fairness and positive attitude among a population that is under exerted stress from various causes. This requires a higher intellect and energy than just kill-ing or torturing. "The Headless Snake" comes from a briefing by the CIA to introduce the Phoenix Program concept; if you cut the head off a snake, the snake dies. Using this faulted theory that by killing the VC leadership we can win the war was a mistaken strategy that murdered thousands of Vietnamese as suspects without cause. The program was counterproductive and a failure.

I had results from numerous field operations to develop a strategy (Persuasion with Relevance) that would reduce the loss of lives, property, and determine the essential factors necessary to influence a population to support a less violent settlement of conditions. Working within the Phoenix Program, I was going one way while the primary effort of the program was going the opposite. This had a personal cost for me.

The results of these field experiences, especially working Chieu Hoi in developing Psychological Operations for Phoenix, produced Persuasion with Relevance, a strategy to influence indigenous populations to support one side rather than another and reduce civilian violence or eliminate it in the process. We tested every possible facet of our being in contested enemy territory that would be negative as to our presence there and developed positive influences. The American military was the largest destructive force in destroy-ing civilians, unnecessarily and often.

I don't know how we survived in Vietnam without all the body armor and electronic equipment. The AK47 rifle was the weapon of choice, then as now. The US military now thinks 60 pounds of equipment is necessary for each man on foot. If you showed up at my door so equipped and unannounced, I would probably shoot you. If I lived in a mud hut where wood for doors is impossible to replace and you kicked down my door...I know I would quickly learn how to make an IED (improvised explosive device).

It is my hope a peaceable correction can be made without violence; this solely depends on the transition of the American Military. It is apparent now that the American government, even before 9/11, was plotting to use the military to dominate selected countries for control of resources for profits rather than the claimed ruse of establishing a democracy and improving lifestyles for the people. Hence, the killing of millions of civilians and massive destruction of property was an acceptable cost.

The future is poised to develop more small wars involving violent disputes over control of natural resources and populations. To this future potential situation add the fact that with an open arms supplier world market, there is the possible purchase of the Mach 2.8 surface to surface missile developing as a second generation with a capability of 200 pounds plus warhead and a range of 700 miles. That is not all; it has the option of target visual imagery, or inertial guidance. This means it does not require satellite control or a bomber or war ship to launch; once launched we do not have the ability to stop it. Now think about target options, buildings, military installations, or maybe an atomic storage facility. Persuasion with Relevance should be the peaceful strategy of choice as an initial means to consider to reduce violence and still produce a settlement of adequate means. The message I send to all military: select personnel only from the military ranks and train all personnel as specialists. Understand deployment, security of operations, and command procedures. There are better uses for our military than thrashing around the Middle East. The quicker we are at providing free transparent governments, the lower we are at risk from a revenge-driven enemy we created.

Faith doesn't make things easy; it makes them possible.

How can you have faith in America, the nation that wants to control the world, not for democracy, but for greed and power?

It is the author's contention that America lost its basis as an ideological society based on the Constitution and Bill of Rights during the Vietnam War when Congress failed to act upon their investigation to stop the Phoenix

Program and its murder of 68,000 or more Vietnamese suspects. The pro-gram, without due process in regard to existing law or recognized human rights, authorized torture and murder as acceptable methods. (Note: these murders were of civilian suspects, and not by killing in combat.) Our current political and military leadership has continued to drag us further down from the ideals and leadership that established this government. It is past the time to hold those responsible as accountable to the rule of law so we can return to our heritage of civility and peaceable coexistence. If those responsible are not removed from both political and economic influence, this nation will collapse. Who do you think will pay the consequences for this failure?

JUST WHAT IS THE RESPONSIBILITY OF OUR MILITARY?

The future for American Military is definitely in question; it must adjust to a universal force structure adaptable to meet conditions as they become necessary. It appears the military has found reason to be involved in just about everything. I can understand the need during an enemy attack on the 50 states and during a major natural disaster where the manpower and resources would be needed.

I am concerned about Special Operations in 78 countries with plans to expand to 20 more or our employment of mercenaries to fight for dubious reasons, all without Congressional approval or public debate or oversight of methods and objectives. If it is important enough to be involved, it is important enough to be public. From experience and research of our past adventures in these small wars, the cost in wealth has never been worth it, and the loss of lives and property creates a deep resentment of America that is fertile ground to recruit terrorists against us.

In military terms, "Clear, Hold and Build" is take it or leave it. The military that adopts Persuasion with Relevance will have an advantage in dealing with Third World countries. It is a military strategy but without Search and Destroy, Hunter and Killer, surges, and torture. If you tend to be self-indulgent at other people's expense it will eventually develop into a conflict. If you haven't noticed the basic statistics of our country, we consume more of the earth's resources than any other country. Fair or unfair depends whether you got your share or not.

There is a preponderance of evidence that we have gotten more than our share, primarily because of the two-ocean defense that has isolated us from longitudinal migrations or invasions. Those years of military dominance have been eroded away by technology and the age of rockets that do not require the costly, cumbersome artillery to launch projectiles or aircraft that required expensive support to be able to bomb a target. An honest assessment of the defense of our country, we don't have one.

When one considers we as a people became a nation by violence and preserved itself with a civil war with great violence, it is understandable why we have kept a costly military force as a major part of our heritage, but it is time to change. This country was born with war and has suffered from other wars we deployed our lives and wealth into for questionable reasons and deplorable results. Since 2001 we have plundered several nations that had not caused us harm, spent our blood and wealth with failed results. I have not read of a reason for our failures as could be supplied by the Pentagon. They could be that the condition they have left Iraq and Afghanistan in was their first intention, if they can now claim success.

Is it too much to demand that our government change direction and offer humanitarian help and deploy a peace delegation (Peace Team Forward) before bombs and economic threats? No war has ever been worth the cost in lives and property, when perhaps differences could be settled without violence. We sell arms to the world and finance the cost. Why do we provide the world with the means of violence? The countries that do not buy our arms are listed as potential enemies. If the USA would quit agitating insurgencies all over the world, we might have a chance for a generation or two of peace and prosperity.

We must put our current militaristic departments back in their boxes so we can formulate just what are their objectives. It is past time to do a complete public review of these departments- Military, CIA, State, DHS, TSA, and the performance of the industrial-military complex. We have enough problems home-grown to keep our attention for many years; so, let's get on with the change. It will not come politically; our system has been manipulated and corrupted beyond repair. I have hope that there are within these depart-ments enough Americans to unite and stand their ground based on our Con-stitution. I propose a peaceful, nonviolent transition, but the transition must come soon before rebellion and revolutions can get started because the cur-rent governmental direction is taking away our liberty and freedoms. Persuasion with Relevance is a strategy that can be deployed to reduce or completely avoid the carnage of war; it is worth the effort to prepare for it while realigning our military to meet the coming restrictions to be placed on the cost of the military.

THOUGHTS AND OPINIONS ON COUNTERINSURGENCY (COIN)

With the discovery of counterinsurgency, as opposed to trench warfare, it seems the military has reinvented war. My 1980 dictionary lists "counterin-surgency" as: military and political action carried on to defeat an insurgency. And "insurgent": rising in opposition to governmental or political authority. And "revolution": overthrow of a government or social system

I have ancestors who were insurgents; they fought the British in the American Revolutionary War.

Are the Taliban revolutionists or insurgents?

The nonviolent approaches to settling grievances, common sense and logic should tell you to try them before you start the killing. However, our history is replete with wars, invasions, conquests, genocides, atomic bombs, (the bombing of Japan) etc. With the introduction of impersonal war machinery, human life has become meaningless. Whatever happened to consciousness of good versus evil? Did they invent a new war or just the need for more war machinery and profits from the military industrial complex?

Vietnam history has been rewritten so every career officer or others can say they were part of one of the largest murders of civilians in American history. The reason I say murder is because these civilians were individually named and targeted, executed without trial. All this time the nation of South Vietnam had a functioning civil court system. Many citizens of South Vietnam were targeted on the flimsiest of evidence to embellish the status of security in a MACV sector or to enhance a career. A lesson learned in Vietnam? Based on current stories out of Afghanistan, murder is still legal if the military says so. These small wars with urban population and "no front lines for security" seem to be too difficult for our military to find solutions for their tactics to overcome. History has repeated itself after 45 years since Vietnam.

The current failure of COIN comes from deploying psychological operations improperly and mixing it up with Search and Destroy operations and hoping to gain intelligence from it. I don't want counterinsurgency advertised as a failure because the Americans did not properly use the concept. Psychological operation missions cannot be pushed to accelerate a strategy. The strategy of attacking central insurgent populations to kill off leadership is ambitious but not very realistic with an insurgent enemy.

Counterinsurgency has some type of magical appeal to the military; it has created a whole new field for career minded officers. The attraction of COIN is very strange because to experience it in enemy or insurgent territory assumes a risk few people will take. It is more akin to salesmanship than marksmanship. It has been over-exposed for its own good, if there ever was one. Successes are not supportive of the concept. Its originators seem to have recently faded away. Since COIN is a tactic that has no real history and does not have much to do with expensive war material, anyone can claim their involvement with counterinsurgency development. In Vietnam, I do not recall any reports or briefings on the subject 1966-1968. Since it involved psy-ops, it would have had to pass through our group. There was always activity on destroying the infrastructure support by eliminating those who were involved as enemy combatants.

Having learned to work with and motivate the VC/NVA who defected to the Chieu Hoi Program, I was then assigned to the ICEX-Phoenix Program to develop Psychological Operations via field operations. ICEX was originally developed to pool intelligence information from all the many different sources and establish operating offices in each province and district. I was assigned as the national psy-ops officer for ICEX. The following is the order released to combine the military psy-ops with Chieu Hoi under direction of Harry Wagner, per General Rosson to General Westmoreland.

UNCLASSIFIED

E F T O

S

PRIORITY

CG I FFORCEV NHA RVN

COMUSMACV TSN RVN

E F T O AVFA-CS 6251 . Rosson sends for Westmoreland.

RECEIVED
CORDS REGION II
NHATRANG
10 SEP 1967

1. In order to coordinate more effectively our military PSYOP assets with the civilian PSYOP and Chieu Hoi assets of this headquarters, I have combined my military PSYOP staff (formerly in G-3) and the Chieu Hoi Division of CORDS under direction of Mr. Wagner, Chief of the Chieu Hoi Division.

2. Underlying the decision are the following:

    a. Coordination will be facilitated and direction will be more consistent because a single individual will be responsible for all PSYOPS programs.

    b. The inducement phase of Chieu Hoi Program has the highest priority in PSYOP. Consolidation of all assets will enhance this effort.

    c. CORDS controls the Chieu Hoi, Information, Sector G-2 and Sector S-5 advisors at all levels and influences the Corps and division S-2 and S-5 advisors through DSA II Corps. It is through

TYP 107

DANIEL B. CULLINANE, JR.
Lieutenant Colonel, GS
Secretary of the General Staff

JAMES P. GASTON
Captain, AGC
Assistant Adjutant General

E F T O   UNCLASSIFIED

> UNCLASSIFIED
>
> CG I FFORCEV NHA RVN
>
> these advisors that we influence our Vietnamese counterparts. Integration will permit more effective coordination of the PSYOP efforts thru direct communication with these advisors.
>
> d. The Chieu Hoi Division controls exploitation of Hoi Chanh. The Sector S-2 advisors and province Chieu Hoi personnel are the principal sources of PSYOP "feed back." This reorganization makes these vital sources of information more readily available to the PSYOP Program.
>
> e. The Chieu Hoi Division funding capabilities, which military PSYOP can use to improve its programs, are available only if PSYOP is part of CORDS.
>
> 3. To obviate my one reservation concerning adequate and responsive support of tactical operations, the senior military PSYOP officer will continue to be directly responsible to the G-3.
>
> MFR: Gen Rosson is informing Gen Westmoreland of his reasons for combining the military PSYOP staff and the Chieu Hoi Division of CORDS. Approved by Chief of Staff on 9Sep67.
>
> AVFA-CS   UNCLASSIFIED   E F T O

I had to learn new methods. The results were a very successful strategy, **Persuasion with Relevance**, to be against an enemy insurgency in the govern-ment infrastructure. "Counter" is to oppose, and to the military, that means domination by force; this starts the whole process off wrong. I prefer to call it what it is, Psychological Operations or Persuasion with Relevance.

I was researching methods to train others because I have the experience and knowledge to train and deploy the correct way, the way Persuasion with Relevance is most effective. These units can be a vital addition to any military organization. The universality of these properly trained units capitalizes on human relationships rather than armed dominance, but as the basis of their training, they are an exceptional fighting force when required.

Petraeus was in the ninth grade, McChrystal in the eighth, Kilcullen and Nagi were not born yet; I was 37 and in the enemy's backyard in a Vietnamese hut with a family who had three children in the VC military. At 10 PM I was persuading them to not support the VC and NVA. I did not ask them to do anything for me. I was telling them why I was there and what I liked about Vietnam and the Vietnamese I worked with every day. And someday I would like to come back and stay longer and meet more of their children and friends. The two men who came into the village with me were former VC and Chieu Hoi returnees.

This scene was repeated 100 times 1967-1968, most of the time with units trained with Persuasion with Relevance. We would proceed once we had confirmed intelligence that we would not endanger the villagers in a crossfire if there was opposition. We avoided situations where we would confront a VC or NVA main force; it would serve no purpose in the development of our concept. The biggest danger was from VC arrow patrols; they were fit to fight. The VC patrols had taken many American lives due to poor training on how to react to them.

We learned about the intimidation of the villagers to get compliance or to enforce controls of the VC. These tragedies the military were seldom aware of, some of the most brutal and savage cruelty one can imagine. One of the tactics used was to cut off a hand or foot, with a machete, of children under the age of six. I carried six syringes of morphine so the mother of a mutilated child did not have to smother her child to death to stop it's suffering.

The APTs (Armed Propaganda Teams) wore black; I wore a blue sport shirt and tan slacks, concealed side arm 357 revolver. I used an interpreter; I spoke very little Vietnamese, but understood more, mostly key words. I taped my interpreter frequently and had it translated, not from fear, but to help with phrasing subjects.

One of my translators. She was a college educated woman.

With or without an insurgent problem, you will find that with the capabilities of our trained personnel in this program, you will be requesting more of these trained men. We took the military over the threshold of tradition by reducing their appearance and conduct to a less rigid, authoritative and asserting manner.

This is something that should be further developed based on case-by-case requirements and one that could be the hardest to accomplish. There is a time and place to be protective, no doubt, but the strategy must be persuasion rather than force. Just think about the appearance of a public employee, say a policeman, if his uniform was to look like a robot from outer space; many of the Third World countries have never seen a combat uniform like the Americans now wear confronting them. I repeat, most of these populations read faces for recognition; we call it passive intelligence They see things we don't; they are not aware of it. It is a means of security and survival, but totally oblivious to most Americans. The Teams from Persuasion with

Relevance were trained in recognizing "passive intelligence" and how to exploit it for security.

Persuasion with Relevance is the strategy used to reduce violence and work with the population and not govern them with indifference to their cul-ture, especially as to their family. In our developing of psychological methods, research indicated that cultures with a custom of ancestral worship had strong family ties that must be protected in dealing with them, no exceptions.

Recent photos (April 2013) of drone killings of small children by the American military, (I don't capitalize "military" until they conduct themselves as the American military should) is cruel and unnecessary. Yes, I am critical of the leadership, but I offer better methods and strategies, having been in the military and Vietnam (see my credentials).

In summary, dealing with "insurgency" in today's unsettled conditions will require major changes in how the United States of America sets aside many military traditions and adopts new standards. Their duty is to provide our security, but learn respect for human life, all human life and act accordingly.

My success with people is to see them as survivors...all just survivors until I understand them and can adjust to them as they are.

LOOKING IN THE MIRROR FROM A DIFFERENT VIEW

As a variation of the old saying goes, "Mirror on the wall, who is the most powerful of them all?" When the American military stand in front of a mirror what do they see? They see themselves as the product of the most powerful military force in the world. This I have no problem with, if they correctly understand that on the other side of the mirror the view is most often considerably different for indigenous populations.

I think it is imperative that the military recognizes what they look like to other observers, and the front view of themselves is very revealing in the mirror on the wall. Dressed for combat, there is little to see of the person in uniform. I understand the necessity for this equipment, but there must be a trade-off if the man in the combat uniform is to relate to the local populace.

People, who have no way of identifying who is in front of them but must assume there is danger or the combat uniform would not be needed.

The people's view is from the reality of an occupation and war with the effect it has on their lives. The American military has found that the application of its great power has limits and that the concentration of its power is often diminished by the nature and dimensions of its opponents.

The person in the combat uniform holding a gun with his finger on the trigger; *is he here as an invader, or as a friend...how can I tell? Why is he here? I know that with him comes death and destruction. Why is he free to enter my house and frighten my family?*

I don't know him; he is very different from us, and we know from experience death follows him everywhere. Our lives have been very simple; why are they here, these strange violent men?

What do those on the other side of the mirror see? Not what you see from the front.

I read an article where American Generals were described as the "Peacocks of the Pentagon," though in most cases an unfair comment, but nevertheless, true. I believe the officers have become too pompous. We haven't had a victory parade since V J Day that I can recall.

I did not see the VC officers in parade uniforms, nor the Taliban. I believe our military is officer top heavy.

If we are to deploy outside of our country, we must reveal our presence as to who we are. Are we the super killers or are we human and survivors as others are? If we cannot breathe the air of the populace we occupy, maybe it is best that we not be there.

I fear that the "One World" concept is a lie and is shaping up to be a massive tragedy that will cost lives in the millions Why is our military being used to push this concept? Why?

There is no justification for the current deployment of our military being used as strike forces in countries that are no threat to our security. If this is the new age of the New World Order, it must be stopped and the few people pushing it retired or deported out of government and world affairs. There is nothing, religious or assumed, that has ordained "them" to be in control of all people as they see how and who benefits from earth's resources. Their control is based on violence, enforced by death and destruction. To sustain human life form on earth will require cooperation and not combat as in death and destruction. The plurality of the human life form can survive without the controls of plutocracy or their bureaucrats.

No, it is not a perfect world; but compassion always wins out over any alternatives.

Has the education of our Generals been so neglected these years that they willingly comply with this New World Order and believe the military's primary function is that of war in foreign lands and not defense of our Constitution? Our military's manpower and resources must be realigned to be able to offer more assistance and fewer assassinations.

LIFE IN A CAREERIST GOVERNMENT BUREACRATIC PROGRAM

The situation this country has been maneuvered into by the international criminals has become serious. Our military current condition and past failures, due to a lack of strong, capable leadership and a policy in compliance with our Constitution, has led us to one obvious solution: transition of the military.

The reason I stress the transition of our military is because it has the ability to sustain itself during a transition period.

June 1968, I was directed to attend a meeting at the Embassy, the meeting to decide if an American Division should be sent into Region IV, the Delta. That part of Vietnam is rivers, canals, forests, swamps, and a lot of VC. I was assigned to canvas the Vietnamese population as to their support for such a move. Up to this time, there were no large detachments of Americans in the region. In two weeks, I was to report back with results.

I asked the Vietnamese Regional Commander who to see, no response. I went to a business owner. He said to go to the Chinese bookkeepers; there are several and talk to the patriarch of each clan. I found six of them; all op-posed the idea of an American Division. Then I found retired General Timmie, the MAAG Commander in Vietnam (1950's-1960's). I got an Air America plane and pilot; we spent a whole day flying over the region. He was very knowledgeable of the area as to military problems. He was not in favor of the move.

I reported back to the Embassy meeting, consisting of a General with a couple of other officers, two Embassy officials, and a Rand employee. My suggestion was to put a reinforced ARVN division, not an American. I gave the reasons. The General asked the Rand man; he put a 10-inch stack computer printout on the table.

"We believe our study supports the move; it would be a strong positive deployment."

I asked Rand how long had he been in Vietnam? *Two days in Saigon.* How many days in the Delta? *None.* Most likely the move was to make more stars for some generals.

The General said it was a go. The Embassy men said the request had already been printed but would take at least three weeks to get an appointment with the Vietnamese President. I spoke up, "Give it to me; I will give it to him today." And I could have; I knew President Ky from in the field and socially, no big deal. The room got quiet and the meeting was over. They sent a Division into the Delta...a disaster. The South Vietnamese lost a couple of thousand civilians in the Delta. This brings back heavy memories...

There are some outstanding exceptions to the following statement, but in general, the officers in Vietnam were poorly trained; the enlisted were undisciplined. I rated 14 officers up to and including Lt Colonels and take exception to the system. For civilians, it was always "career enhancement," which equals a mess.

You will find that many of the screw-ups were the result of natural human reaction to the problems created by the circumstances of war. The major exception being the employment of the Phoenix Program Vietnam under the control of the CIA and William Colby, with the murder of thousands of Vietnamese civilians. Once this was accepted as a military tactic by a Congressional investigation, the American government was continued as the world's predominant terrorist. The current use of Hunter Killer Teams to intimidate indigenous populations, along with drone attacks without a direct response to being attacked or confirmed intelligence to support the attack is murder. Phoenix in Vietnam was often tagged as "murder incorporated." Now, most of the world can tag the Americans with that title, with leadership that takes pride in the successful murder and torture of Third World countries. I can attest that torture is more counterproductive than productive using government to advance their personal interests and profits.

How soon till the government turns their guns on us?

I believe that our Declaration of Independence and Constitution are the most valuable documents ever produced to guarantee liberty and freedom for all Americans.

Are we so stupid to allow anyone to take that away from us?

On several MACV inspection trips the USAID Regional Director and CG of MACV were asked by at least four Vietnamese Province Chiefs, *what do you want?* Answer, *More Wagner's*. The Army CG Rosson took this for a plus, and we worked closely on many things. The USAID Regional Director's secretary, who took notes for reports on these inspections, always kept me aware of my involvement. She let me read the reports they had. As a career bureaucrat, the credit should have gone to the Regional Director. If he was informed, he would have been involved. If the military and CIA weren't reporting our joint activities, for security reasons I couldn't.

Being successful and not part of the career USAID or CIA/ CORDS managerial hierarchy, success could mean a ticket out of Vietnam. 25 years later, I met a fellow USAID vet who told me that my personnel problems with USAID came from William Colby building his power personnel pyramid at CORDS.

I would guess that I was the only civilian in Vietnam who talked face to face with North Vietnamese officers in South Vietnam about defecting over to our side and lived to tell about it. This was encompassed by an operation I was assigned to by Ambassador Komer and funded by a White House impress fund of *four million dollars*.

Who else, because of deficient paperwork, with an operational staff of only one Vietnamese and one Chinese who spoke little or no English, was building relationships with defectors? CORDS was all built on a paper empire that failed. The projects I took over were failing or had failed because of too much paper and staff work (reports, meetings, and briefings) and no field work or follow up in the field.

I went to the problems and corrected them before I could report them. It seems that the civilian officer in charge (CORDS) could not maneuver me into their pyramid of power. I cut paperwork, got results. Those who wanted credit for it, they were too close to safety to go out and exploit it themselves. My first lecture in becoming a VIP briefer at the quarterly commander's confer-ence made the point, "We never expose our dirty laundry; always show the good side. Rule number one of a government employee: speak the line, not the truth." A major war was being built on lies, why?

I was working within the Chieu Hoi compounds where we had up to 25 NVA; at least five were officers, one a captain who possibly had gotten me a pass saving my life a couple of times. Vietnamese Police Special Branch picked up a VC who had a camera and several pictures of me and my quarters in Nha Trang, (the Chieu Hoi offices). During the Tet offensive, 16 VC were removed from my quarters. Was I being targeted? At one point I met with two NVA officers; it turned out one was an advisor to the PLA (People's Liberation Army). On a trip to China in 1996, I had an invitation to meet two retired Chinese PLA Generals, one of them being the young officer from Vietnam.

We were not "Rambo," and I did not go to Vietnam to die. My intelligence was good and I believe I took few risks. Believe it or not, I met some nice people...and they met an American different from others. Nonmilitary. Yes, I made some dreadful mistakes, but I learned insurgency of VC and NVA. These forays provided the needed intelligence as to where to deploy my field operations in the developing Psychological Operations.

The loss of lives in Iraq bothers me. The influence the military has, the military budget, and from experience the recognition of the weakness of some of our military programs is problematic. I do have observations and opinions

We know with the rise of the Chinese PLA, the profusion of weaponry worldwide, the increasing sophistication of light infantry weapons, and the increasing imbalance of standards of living among the world's population that warfare no longer fills the needs.

I think we have lived in such an affluent and secure society we have lost the human survival instincts that the population of the Third World survives with every day and night. Our military doesn't understand this; that is why I say the intelligence is in front of them and they can't see it. Whose fault is this, certainly not the civilians who are being killed every day?

THE FOLLOWING IS AN EXAMPLE OF A TYPICAL MILITARY CIVIC ACTION

It was the rainy season in Binh Dinh Province, and the intelligence net we had established in the area had been very active, supported by former Chieu Hoi returnees; then it had stopped completely. Getting out to MACV Sector Headquarters, the roads were a muddy mess. As we came into the village area we passed a building freshly painted yellow, with white trim and a manicured landscape, a Catholic Church. The upkeep was compliments of the US military.

Going a little further in the rain and mud we passed three Buddhist monks standing beside the road under an umbrella with their begging bowl; they were covered with mud. I had the driver pull off the road so we could watch the monks. Every military vehicle that passed by the monks made an effort to splash them with mud and water, and you could see that the Americans thought it was funny. I instructed the driver to go by the local Buddhist Grotto; it was falling apart since a tree had crashed through the roof. We then headed to the MACV Sector Headquarters to find the Civic Action Officer.

Captain (O'Reilly?) was his name, and I explained to him that only 2% of the population formed that church. They were mostly from North Vietnam and supported the French more than the Americans. The majority of the population was Buddhists. Alienating that many people would dry up useful information from the 98% of the people who were not members of the Catholic Church.

I would return in two weeks to see how the Buddhist temple looked, and it better look very good with a lot of smiling monks when I get there.

A small lesson, but important, because it was absolutely necessary to keep our intelligence net active in a heavily populated area.

Everything the Americans think is right, and the indigenous population must adapt to the "American Way" is a nice idea, but definitely not true.

It would take 6 to 12 months of my time to reestablish reliable intelligence sources in the area because I was the only direct connection to the Vietnamese link with integrity and stable intelligence sources.

HAMLET EVALUATION WORKSHEET

Following page is the MACV device to tally the state of security in South Vietnam. These completed forms were totaled in a report for MACV monthly and reported to Washington. Two USAID senior members did a study as to their accuracy. One of them, Colonel Lloyd Wills, said the only thing that was accurate was the scheduling of the US officers' rotation of duty. Officer rotat-ing out, (the sector was very peaceful); new officer rotating in, (the sector was in enemy control). In fact, we did not know the real status of most of the country.

HAMLET EVALUATION WORKSHEET*

●

DIRECTIONS FOR COMPLETING HAMLET EVALUATION WORKSHEET: All hamlets are to be evaluated except those that are considered by the subsector evaluator to be under VC control. It is suggested that a separate Worksheet be used for each evaluated hamlet. During the month, update the evaluation and the problem responses as necessary. At the end of the month review the worksheets. It is recommended that the response selected for each of the 18 indicators be entered in the righthand column. Entries that differ from those made in the preceding month should be transferred to the Hamlet Evaluation Summary Form (HESF) for transmittal to MACV in Saigon. If worksheet entries are made in pencil, the same form can be used repeatedly.

1. Identify the hamlet by name and location at the top of the Worksheet. Type of hamlet refers to RD Plan hamlet types: Ap Doi Moi (ADM), Ap Tan Sinh (ATS), Ap Cung Co (ACC), or Ap Binh Dinh (ABD). Use a check mark to indicate whether or not the hamlet is in a National Priority Area (NPA). Enter the best available population figure and indicate by a check mark whether the figure is reliable or unreliable. A reliable figure would fall within 10% of an accurate head count in the opinion of the subsector evaluator. Use a check mark to record that the hamlet has been visited during the month by a US District Team member or other designated US personnel and/or by a member of the GVN District staff.

2. For each of the 18 indicators, select the response that best represents the hamlet conditions during the month. The brief responses given on the Worksheet are intended to suggest steps in progress from E to A. Refer to Joint MACV-OCO Directive 1-67, 2 Jan 67, Annex E, Guidance for Evaluating HES, for more complete discussion. It should be understood that within each indicator, signs of progress in one rating, "D" for example, are implied in a related "C" rating if not repeated in the description of the "C" rating. The responses refer to the hamlet itself unless otherwise stated.

3. Enter in the boxes at the far right the number that represents the confidence you have in the validity of the information upon which your ratings for each factor were based: (1) No confidence; (2) Low confidence; (3) Medium confidence; (4) High confidence; (5) Complete confidence.

4. Changes in the wording of indicators are printed in upper case.

HAMLET PROBLEMS DURING MONTH

Select the one best answer for each section of each question

1. Incidents of misconduct by friendly elements adversely affecting friendly relations with the hamlet populace:
   a. US Military. ☐ 1. None; ☐ 2. Minor only; ☐ 3. Serious; ☐ 4. Inapplicable; ☐ 5. Unknown
   b. Other FWMAF ☐ 1. None; ☐ 2. Minor only; ☐ 3. Serious; ☐ 4. Inapplicable; ☐ 5. Unknown
   c. ARVN ☐ 1. None; ☐ 2. Minor only; ☐ 3. Serious; ☐ 4. Inapplicable; ☐ 5. Unknown
   d. RF/PF ☐ 1. None; ☐ 2. Minor only; ☐ 3. Serious; ☐ 4. Inapplicable; ☐ 5. Unknown
   e. RD Team ☐ 1. None; ☐ 2. Minor only; ☐ 3. Serious; ☐ 4. Inapplicable; ☐ 5. Unknown

2. Actions by friendly elements during military operations adversely affecting relations with hamlet populace: (including but not limited to fire from any type of weapon, destructive passage within hamlet area, defoliation)
   ☐ 1. None;
   ☐ 2. Minor only.
   ☐ 3. Serious
   ☐ 4. Unknown.

3. Corruption or tyranny of hamlet or village officials:
   ☐ 1. No indications
   ☐ 2. Rumored.
   ☐ 3. Suspected but no proff.
   ☐ 4. Solid indication.
   ☐ 5. Unknown.

Continued on page 3.

CHAPTER 2

PERSUASION WITH RELEVANCE

A MODERN MILITARY STRATEGY

PSYCHOLOGICAL OPERATIONS

This book is the sum and substance of my experiences in Vietnam 1966-1968 and years of research into the military operations in Iraq and Afghanistan.

War is hell.

I believe in these times that a strong and technologically advanced military is essential, not to dominate foreign populations over political differences or territorial claims, but to secure the safety of the North American continent.

I believe that physiologically humans are by nature perishable but not expendable.

A modern military so equipped has the resources of manpower and organization to provide a kaleidoscope of service to the world other than dispersing death and destruction as its primary objective.

Psychological Operations as a military strategy as described in this book far outweighs the current alternative. The approach is a military concept and not a "peace-nik" adventure. It is using your head and not your fist to outmaneuver any opponent by using military armament for security as and when needed while resolving conflicts peacefully.

WE ARE MILITARY MEN WITH A MISSION

"The Air We Breathe" means learning by getting close to your "opponents" as opposed to the dead air of lectures, classrooms, manuals, and so-called experts with little or no first-hand experience or with blood on their hands having met the enemy.

METHODOLOGY

The branch of logic concerned with the application of the principles of reasoning to scientific and philosophical inquiry.

PSYCHOLOGY

The science dealing with the mind and with mental and emotional processes; the sum of the actions, traits, attitudes, thoughts, mental states, etc., of a person or group.

PSYCHIATRY

The branch of medicine concerned with the study, treatment, and prevention of disorders of the mind, including psychoses and neuroses, emotional maladjustments, etc.

EXPLANATION OF THE THEORY OF CONFLUENCE STRATEGY

After all the research over the last many years and over 30,000 pages of research material in preparation for this book, it all comes down to the fact my psychological field operations produced the applicable strategy. All of the so-called experts on counterinsurgency have at least one (there are others) critical flaw in their concept of the deployment of the manpower to resist insurgent advances. COIN is as deployed the wrong image, that of a subversion of local culture and loyalties and controls enforced by military dominance. The military has made changes, but so far has for the most only changed nomenclature.

It is not the purpose of this book to criticize any one individual's work but to make the point those 22 months and the 30 field operations I controlled in Vietnam had produced a concept that puts the emphasis on personnel, train-ing, and tactics, as well as deployment. The differences are explained in this book.

This outline of the concept put to use in the field in Vietnam is explained by these features:

Sheath (enemy*)
- Reasons and conditions for existence
- Cultural
- Final objective of the enemy

*The enemy as insurgents, infrastructure, invaders, or terrorists

Spear Team (the introductory asset)
- Selection of Team personnel
- Training of personnel
- Environmental and passive intelligence
- Indigenous personnel training
- Command control
- Strategy
- Tactics
- Objectives

Shield Team (security)
- Army units matched to enemy capabilities
- Communications
- Strategy vs terrain
- Reserves
- Logistics

There are imperatives to this type warfare that the Pentagon has ignored leading to a failed mission. Two of the essential elements for success are collection of the right environmental intelligence and preparation training of specially selected and trained military as a start in developing the Teams applicable to Psychological Operations.

"Counterinsurgency" is nothing but a name and is being used to popularize the small wars the Americans keep provoking for economic and political purposes.

THE CONFLUENCE OF STRATEGY

Psychological methods as adverse to death, torture, and property destruction will never be successful if cultural aspects and lifestyle conditions are not brought together at a level as improvements that are popularized and sustainable by the population.

Military actions used to induce foreign dominance and for control, result-ing in profits or for territorial security of one of the activists will never be suc-cessful. The approaches will differ as to technique.

There is a monstrous amount of information available about history on wars of aggression. For some reason, history is replete with famous Admirals and Generals from wars of aggression and the bigger the actions, the greater the glory. I cannot say that attacks and counterattacks of great nations were right or wrong. History shows that most were a huge waste of wealth and lives, and the tipping point that started them is never really clearly understood.

The differences of geography, resources, and climate vary worldwide and can bring about disagreements between neighbors or between the diversity of populations. Unfortunately, these differences blossom into aggressive actions and aggressive reactions.

Is there a better non-violent way to resolve these problems? Yes, but it takes special planning and trained personnel with a strategy for timely deployment of forces and trained Teams.

In order to visualize the ideal deployment, we illustrated with the action of water in a stream. Sounds simple, it is simple; it illustrates deployment strategy.

We start with the source and from it, gravity forces the water downhill as a small stream.

(The stream seeks the point of less resistance and concentrates its force rather than spreading out and weakening the force to overcome obstructions in its path).

The development of learning initially from smaller groupings, the ability to appear with less dominance as techniques are improved upon the Teams, developing confidence with successes and adjusting to conditions.

(As the stream proceeds on its way it learns from the smaller and easier ways to overcome obstacles).

The Teams are now learning and working well and adjusting their tactics, gaining wider and better intelligence about the opponent (enemy).

(The stream is now becoming organized as it grows larger and moving faster but still not spreading out too far from its main course).

The actions of the Teams are now becoming recognized as a threat to the enemy and resistance is beginning to build as other groupings are beginning to show signs of approval of the Teams' work.

(The stream is now moving into different courses to spread out as it pushes further ahead, always improving and advancing its strategy to advance on a wider front).

The enemy is now losing support populations and resources and must reclaim as much as possible. To do so must commit resources from the base camps and larger population centers to react to the Teams' advances.

Before you can surge to overcome larger obstructions, there must be the presence of a successful solution that is less threatening and provides a better living style resulting from less violent military actions.

The strategy is attacking the enemy on a wider front with the options of where next to insert more Teams. The Shield Teams are looking for opportunities to counter any aggression of the enemy that cannot concentrate its forces without giving up more resources to the other advancing Teams.

A part of the strategy is to earn the trust of the indigenous, with improvements to the new groupings made available and culturally acceptable. They should be projects that are labor intensive for the population functioning around family awareness, and providing for food and water, shelter, and security.

The design of all improvements must include the cooperation and organization of the local population with the Spear Team's guidance, with Peace Team Forward as mentors.

The Shield Teams must provide security from aggression and support the Spear Teams when necessary; however, the Spear Team must organize to respond to local police-type problems by involving indigenous personnel.

The analogy to the stream is for instructional purposes, to illustrate the concept as opposed to the "surge." In every case the actual terrain and population must be studied to develop the strategy before the deployment.

Primarily due to the development of intelligence gathering systems and weaponry, the massing of large battle groups is over. The current trend of Hunter-Killer Teams (Special Operations, Special Forces, and Seals) to eliminate enemy leadership will reach a point where the defense of them will be to retaliate in kind. The Hunter-Killer Teams and now drones are a zero-sum gain and ultimately could become a high-risk strategy.

The Persuasion with Relevance strategy can be readily adapted to meet requirements of the population, culture, terrain, weather, and force required of the mission.

Of course, this is the basic illustration of the concept and in practice, a lot of data must be gathered and analyzed for initial deployment and in preparation for following deployments.

A SUMMARY OF THE SHEATH, SPEAR, AND SHIELD, STRATEGY, AND TACTICS OF PERSUASION WITH RELEVANCE AS DEVELOPED IN VIETNAM

The changes in governments, immigration, insurgency, or cultural differences are all the possible environments for the psychological concept of the "Sheath, Spear, and Shield." The purpose of this concept is to reduce the destructiveness of the combat between the military and the enemy or insurgency that is in opposition to it. This concept has been repeatedly tested successfully when applied in applicable situations by properly trained person-nel at the most advantageous tactical time. It is more effective if introduced before general hostilities develop and with a thoroughly planned strategy adequately supported by personnel and resources. It is not the one-tactic-solves-all solution and should stand as one approach, not a party to main force aggression.

THE SHEATH: We refer to the "Sheath" as standing for the insurgency, enemy, or supporting infrastructure. This is to symbolize that it cannot be crushed to resolve it but must be dealt with as a total problem. An insurgency is typically based upon a segment of the population with a grievance against an authority that has not been adequately settled, resulting in hostilities. To attempt to crush the Sheath without first determining whether there is a legitimate basis for it to be active is counterproductive. Confronting the insurgency is like determining the contents of an egg without breaking the shell; one starts with the origin of the egg and the influences that prevailed in its creation. The military is too often stuck on operations that crush the egg and produce a lot of explosions and body counts. Efforts should be made to have it subverted to a less hostile outcome. To hastily attempt to crush the insurgency resulting in causalities gives it additional strength to exist. Rule number one: Know your insurgency. In the world today, everyday hostilities are possible.

THE SPEAR: The "Spear" are the specially trained personnel who will advance into the territory that is in dispute with the insurgency. The Spear Team is trained to adapt to problems; civil, natural disasters, as well as military by being able to be self-sufficient and not an added burden to local infrastructure. Although the Teams are very adaptive, they generally have a single mission: to convert negative or neutral populations into a positive, supportive attitude and to accomplish this without force. The key to this con-cept is the special selection and training of the Spear personnel; their training is determined by the necessity to be accepted by the members of the population allied to the insurgents. This has a lot to do with cultural and habitat conditions; learn not to aggrieve by reason of cultural or traditional mistakes that would offend. I found through trial and error that the rural personnel adapted better to the training than did city personnel, and non-commission officers did better than commission officers This was partially due to the generalist abilities associated with rural living.

This is to note that not all encounters will be friendly, and a demonstration of strength could be necessary to indicate the Spear Team's determination to be recognized. The Spear Team by necessity must have a military posture for their security but a much less *appearance* as military. The real military capability force is the Shield Team. Every situation will be different, that is why special personnel and training are necessary. Training is essential to show correct and proper presence, communication, and to develop passive intelligence to determine the best reconciliation of issues. I found that I had to spend more time teaching Team members to recognize what they were seeing as valuable intelligence and how to assemble it into important advantageous information.

The objective is to force the enemy or insurgents to disperse to recover lost territory, population, and resources as the Spear and Shield Teams begin to spread out and take control of population centers with nonviolent tactics where possible. Start on the periphery where exposure is somewhat limited and begin choosing smaller populations to test your concept and issues. Work around the larger population centers (don't bypass them).

The point must be made that an overall strategy be mapped out and support organized to approach as illustrated by: A label stuck in the center of a sheet of paper, to remove it there are two methods. One, attack the center of it to release it totally from the paper. This almost always fails. The second method is to start on the periphery of the label and begin to loosen it bit by bit around the perimeter, working constantly toward the center until the label is removed. This method denies the enemy or insurgent the ability to keep his force concentrated and sustainable as resources are being removed. It weakens the enemy forces and keeps them distracted trying to preserve territory and population support being removed by the Spear Teams. The faster you move Teams in successfully, the weaker and more dispirited the main force becomes and the more support your side develops.

Of course, there can be encounters with violence, but that is what the Shield is for.

THE SHIELD: This is the typical military strength force with the capability to overcome any aggression toward the Spear Team. The composition of this force depends on the need to take advantage of terrain to dominate the approaches to the Spear Team's location. Obvious fact- nothing always goes as planned and alternatives must be readily called into action in order to minimize any reaction against the Spear Team.

The Shield will be located as not to impose military dominance on the population while the Spear Team is working successfully. The Shield Team can be aggressive in minimizing any militant signs of counteraction against the Spear Team. We recognize this is not Sunday School, and actions and counter-actions must be anticipated and be dealt with quickly and to emphasize the determination to resolve any and all grievances peacefully.

From the above descriptions, the tactics are planned to erode the fringe populations away from the control of the insurgents and keep advancing to take more and more population and resources away from the insurgent central control. If possible, weaken the main forces so they can be engaged in negotiations or destroyed.

It is not a perfect world and early deployment, constant pressure, open negotiations, promises made and kept, integrity, and security all contribute to successful operations.

The operational guidelines we refer to as **"PTA."** Planning, Training, Attitude. The resources to be determined by each situation but always include as needed by observation- medical, food, and tools for distribution by the

Team. There are some guideposts; the Spear Team should be comprised ideally for every one Team member a minimum of five indigenous members, all specifically trained for the deployment. In major problem areas, the Team members should be on assignment no less than 18 months. Trust and relationships are best remembered by affiliating memory to specific seasons, birthdays, weddings, and deaths, etc. It is just human nature, the way we react. The training emphasizes these cultural and natural traits for each specific population and the grievances driving the insurgency hostilities.

The command structure is different; the Spear Team leader will make all the operational decisions going up the normal chain of command in most circumstances, and his appearance and operational conduct will be more ob-served as civilian than military. This must be clearly understood by the higher commands. Note that the entire tactical plan was agreed upon before de-ployment. This requires the indoctrination of all area military command and resources as to the Spear Team existence, requirements, and priorities.

The most critical problem that usually develops is the removal of the "thugs" who attach themselves to most insurgencies and are infiltrated into the population. These are the militants who show no respect for life and are constantly attempting to build reputation via violence and cruel intimidation when given the opportunity. This is a contest over policy and control and has the potential to quickly become violent. These thugs are usually the precursor for the opposition and must be quickly recognized and made to disappear. The disposal of them must be swift and silent; there are methods that will be covered in training. With a determined enemy, you cannot be assured they will not generate violence.

How, What, Where, When, and How Much? All because I believe there is a better way to deal with localized problems. This is the "Sheath" of contention. The requirement to study, analyze, discuss, evaluate, seek alternatives and agreement is using intelligence and logic. If the Sheath is illegal, unlawful, or contrary to government decree, then engage it with the Spear and Shield to remove the problem via negotiation if possible, by force if needed. If there is a rational grievance let the Spear solve the problem as peacefully as possible using the required resources. The Spear is to correct problems as they are confronted and this may require specialized personnel and material added to the solution; this should be done only after the Spear has stabilized the situation.

We have addressed this material as for a small-scale operation; the same principles apply regardless of size of population. Our field operations in Vietnam's largest operation was a population of 650. Larger populations can be divided into neighborhoods or groupings.

This program is adjustable to fit any size operation and with any cultural group.

There is more to training, covering the gathering of intelligence that most would overlook, showing presence, gesturing, food, children, elderly, clothing, etc....

I have researched all of this and tested it successfully. I have spent more days in the field in unsecured territory working against the insurgency (VC) and the military (NVA) probably than any American at that time in that war. Eighteen months of field operations and tests in the real climate of an active enemy and insurgency of a well-established military; we learned from our mistakes. My time was spent working for solutions, to understand concepts, methods, motivation, weakness, and strengths of insurgence war versus the conventional military maneuver and assault. The Vietnam War was our first major encounter with an insurgency organized and supported by a larger adversary (China and Russia) to our military interference in support of one side of a nationalist movement. Due to my unique position and ability to work with the Vietnamese, I was free to follow my own intuition and marshal the re-sources. I needed to work against the insurgency within their own base areas. The objective was to deny them the hamlets and villages they needed for support. I learned and developed the concept. We advanced the operational concept of where we were successful. We found that the unpredictable is the norm and to be prepared for it and to capitalize on your ability to deal with it successfully when confronted.

These psychological operations are not a supplement to a Search and Destroy main force strategy but *is the strategy*; the main force is committed when the population concedes to its need. There are techniques for applying this concept to urban populations that are different from the typical or normal military methods of cordon and search that were also proven to be an applicable improvement.

If there is a primary consideration to this concept, it is deploying early with trained personnel with a complete strategy.

Again, my desire has always been to minimize violence and reduce the unnecessary loss of lives and property in these ever-increasing uprisings. "Counter" insurgency is and has been promoted as part of the destruction of population by force (we concede that in some circumstance this may be necessary) but remains the least desirable due to the problems of dealing with the aftermath (Iraq and Afghanistan).

We pose a simple question: "Wouldn't it have been better all round and cheaper to have resolved the reasons they keep blowing up trucks rather than trying to build trucks they can't blow up?"

The United States has lost its ability to lead in this type conflict, for numerous reasons, most prominent has been the failures in deployment. It is my hope that the people of USA with its history will recognize and accept the lead in this concept of localized warfare.

The introduction of this concept to training military personnel advances the opportunity for less violent and more often (conceded not always univer-sally successful, we are not quite there yet) agreeable, peaceful settlements of differences with military precision and civilian methods and appearances.

This particular training has a similarity to disaster relief operations; the Spear Team is in its simplest form a unique public administration. Teams not committed could ideally supplement disaster relief efforts or other public problems. They can be current in their military responsibilities.

There is still much to be learned about retraining and the universal utility of this concept of a military organization being accepted by conventional military commands. Yet, as far as can be seen into the future there is still a need for the conventional, old-fashioned military with its armament. However, with increasing world populations, resources could become objects for aggression. As quaint as it may sound, still "earning their trust" through peaceful cooperative or nonviolent psychological operations has all the advantages over any alternatives at this time.

Why do I champion this concept; because of the strong traditional status of the heavily structured power base of the traditional military mindset. To convince them that to redirect their missions with other duties is more beneficial to their future than aggression or conflict. But this shall not detract from their vital mission of defense of the country as a primary mission. Their pomp and circumstance are still their necessary signature appearance. I believe the universality of this concept is the future of ground force military, along with a different organization and command structure.

This description has been simplified for this book, the essential points of the concept.

Psychological Operations are not family counseling.

Psychological Operations are not propaganda.

Psychological Operations are not determining or instructing how to torture humans.

Psychological Operations are not properly deployed as cover for other aggressive tactics.

Psychological Operations are properly deployed to inform others as to the benefits that are available from other interests.

Psychological Operations must have the integrity to provide for the promises it makes in its deployment.

Psychological Operations are built on cultural relationships; military destroys these relationships.

Psychological Operations recognize that no two persons are identical; society is based on family and habitat. These are two of the primary factors in the development of culture.

South Vietnamese propaganda team giving speeches for the government at a small hamlet.

It was one of my objectives in Vietnam to focus my effort on making contact with the opponent in an attempt to work out a solution to stop the mutilation of children to enforce VC demands for village support.

It was the theme I used to meet the North Vietnamese Officer and the PRC Chinese Advisor.

The violence of war with the loss of lives and property has never settled anything worth the cost of war.

Winning their hearts and minds, nope; I want to "earn their trust" and what they have to share will follow.

Fancy slogans are worthless if you cannot deliver the improvements as promised.

Are you making the right moves?

Do you have their attention?

The Peace Team Forward concept of Persuasion with Relevance strategy as deployed is non-military in appearance. It has been tested and developed in a war zone with success and is the practical stability and sustainment solution.

Not the military field manual approach.
Peace Team Forward.
Gets nonviolent results.

THE AMERICAN WAY

In the 44 years since I left Vietnam, I have viewed the aggressiveness of our military in locations that I find it impossible to reason why we are committing our wealth and blood. Based upon our own military reports and those of various news services, the cost is tremendous, and the destruction of properties unbelievable; again, for what? Then there is the taking of non-combat civilian lives by the thousands; again; for what? and the massive destruction of property to gain total dominance of the people; again, for what? There are two views on why. One, it is to protect our United States of America; however, the logic here is a falsehood because there is no linkage. Two, it is to protect a foreign population from the abuse of other governments or their own government. And just why is that our responsibility; to inflate the size of the military and the military suppliers and contractors by using peaceful intent enforced by war. International laws and courts should make these decisions. Our Constitution sets forth that foreign wars and treaties require the support of the American people through the public action of their representatives in Congress, not on Wall Street or the White House. To do otherwise is a treasonable offense.

Due to habitat, geological position, natural resources, culture, genetics, etc....however evolved or created, it is impossible to make an ethical adjustment as to the parity between all nations to serve under one controlling group. (With the singular exception that we all submit to slavery). We must learn to look at all people as "survivors," not poor or rich, and learn to associate; from some of the poorest inhabitants of villages in Vietnam, China, and Latin America I have met some of the nicest, gracious, and sharing people.

From January 1967 till I left Vietnam, I was on call to two White House and CIA agents; I was assigned to clean up specific problems and report results about the problems. The agents, in turn, reported directly to the White House. These agents came to my quarters one night in 1966 in Nha Trang and said they wanted me to work for them, CIA, and out of the Embassy; I appar-ently had no choice.

I did have a lot of good contacts in the military, knew my way around the Vietnamese, civil and military, and was familiar with the whole country. I was told to attend specific briefings and meetings in the Embassy that always ended up requiring field research. Sometimes I was told to take whatever measures were needed in the field to stop or correct them; my efforts were not to be challenged by anyone. I was never in a position to make policy, but in the field, I did maneuver around it occasionally. Mr. Ernest Sparks was the CIA representative for II Corp; he and I worked well together and had much success because of our mutual cooperation.

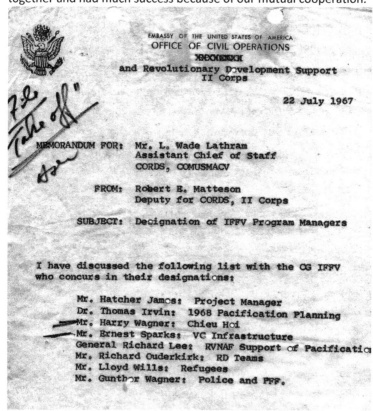

In my other work in military intelligence, Psychological Operations, and Phoenix, I could use my connections as well for their assignments. I was instructed to sit in on several meetings in the Embassy; to travel, it seemed from one end to the other of Vietnam, after Tet '68 to count the dead of the enemy country-wide. This was to verify the numbers published before any count was made. There is no way an accurate count could be made; however, the military did publish a detailed count they obviously concocted for the record. The initial count made public by the White House was 35,000 enemy. I disagreed with that count from actually counting bodies and questioning local Vietnamese.

The White House wanted a North Vietnamese unit to defect with an officer to South Vietnam.

Ambassador Bob Komer said, "Wagner can get one; give him the assignment and funding." This was getting into the possibility of high risk adventure. NVA units were not readily available, and the North had a very tight control of their people. The funding was four million American dollars from White House impress fund as approved by the President. The impress fund was to be used in psy-ops to allow me to increase pressure on the VC and NVA. It was to be used to support the program with all of the military units in the field. I was in contact and conversation with two North Vietnamese officers in 1967. Later I found out one of the officers was a Chinese Army Political Affairs officer to the NVA. Komer knew I had been doing some things and my ability to motivate Vietnamese; some of my intelligence on enemy activity had been exceptional. Personal ratings with the Vietnamese always brought me up as top rated.

This fits in with my psy-ops field operations; it was just deeper into enemy territory where no American had been before. I actually met with two NVA officers several times in their territory; I got two Viet Cong military units to defect and had a North Vietnamese Platoon on the way when they canceled the program for fear of being blamed for exploiting them unethically.

Other than those assignments with the military, I think most were to obtain answers to questions coming into the White Houses and were forwarded to the Embassy for clarification or information. Many of the assignments were of atrocities to investigate from reports being circulated in the States. It was all interesting and more than a little unusual. However, it did give access to a lot of the CIA contacts. The CORDS restructure of the USAID civilian personnel into the control of the military command provided me with the staff rank of General (IFFV Commander Rosson set the rank as a Major General so I would have equal access to all field commanders) and access to any military reports and units as required, as well many briefings of the command staff without question. You will find descriptions of some of these assignments in the Events section of this book.

WASHINGTON, WE HAVE A PROBLEM HERE!

I am not satisfied with conditions and conduct of our government and our military, as it is obvious they use the means of fighting world terrorism as the possible excuse for destroying our Constitutional government. The American Military Way, there is no doubt we bring the terrorists' threats on ourselves with our politically driven, hegemonic military desires of world dominance and for the USI (United States Incorporated) and the elite. Our aggression, arming non-state military forces, drones, killer squads, and torture of suspects and POWs has marked us as being, without moral or legal basis, an evil government. I have not heard of the reason we have military special-ops personnel in 173 countries. *I assume protecting our borders?*

Except for the possibility they are infiltrating targeted countries to gain influence and control of commerce and resources; it really isn't to establish democracy, now is it? Is there a connection to the recent discovery that NSA spying has and continues to supply intelligence providing leverage in gaining control of the targeted? I have been researching the recent efforts of the military at Leavenworth and Carlisle to revise the counterinsurgency concept. All that I have read is fine but still does not take the fundamental critical step necessary to effect change by stepping over the threshold of the traditional military resistance to change the pre-combat situation successfully; one needs only to look at Iraq and Afghanistan missions and the post deployment to see what is wrong with our Department of Defense. In order to be success-ful as a full spectrum military, a realignment of mission and personnel must be attained while still maintaining full combat capability, which it isn't; and future budget cuts can only make it worse.

In the 30 field operations developed for the Phoenix Program in Vietnam against an unrestricted population, we were successful in developing and testing a strategy against a well-organized enemy force by developing the ability to secure the support of the indigenous population. This was accomplished by using "passive environmental intelligence" and the proper "presence" of our Spear Teams.

PASSIVE INTELLIGENCE

All humans and most animals are immersed in passive intelligence; it is a natural function of survival.

Research of the writings on counterinsurgency- none covered the subject of what I refer to as environmental intelligence. All Team members must be trained to increase their powers of observation, and from experience I developed teaching methods. I don't know how they do it, but the general population knows things it doesn't realize it knows. I assume this knowledge is part of surviving in these populations being ravished by war. They view what is considered normal and what is not normal in their surroundings and are not conscious of it, but sub-consciously react to it, and to us, these decisions are intelligence and necessary in sustaining our presences. Find a way to intercept their decisions so you can benefit from knowing the normal from the not normal surroundings.

Every member of a population group knows everyone's face and reads their faces. Of the American urban populations, 1 of 1,000 can read faces for meaning. There is science to this, as facial muscles react to different thoughts and stimuli. You are born with it, but we in the urban areas don't let it develop for lack of need. However, if you're in a lesser developed population the more likely you need to learn what are the natural tendencies in secular motives for the population.

Interpersonal (people) skills are how one reads the emotions of another by how their body reacts to stimuli. In most Third World populations, reading faces is just part of being alive, whereas in the more industrialized populations it is more or less not necessary. Yes, we see happiness and anger but no notice to the small passive signs that fleetingly shoot past us anywhere there are people. Our faces react to our mental reactions without us knowing it We survive in an environment where such actions are not necessary, assuming our security does not require it.

But in other civilizations, the necessity to survive often depends upon knowing friend or foe and constantly being on the alert for danger. There are many obvious signs we display, but there are others that pass with much less recognition or notice in passing. Body language is universal but has almost been lost in many population groups, especially in urban areas.

There is, and have been, university studies of brain functions that indicate facial muscles react subconsciously by stimuli. Reading faces has gained more interest in psychological studies, such areas as interrogations and intelligence gathering. It is a skill that not all persons can develop, that is why the Spear Team members (Persuasion with Relevance) must be selected carefully; this is one military program where individuality counts and not training the herd.

In my tour as a psy-ops officer in Vietnam, one of several responsibilities I learned was to read and communicate with Vietnamese with proper expressions more so than with my deplorable attempts with their language. (And of course, I had a very good interpreter). Very young children detect emotion early and react to it; I believe from observation all children are born with a common language but are taught out of it. Some studies believe it is man's first language, and it is inherited but lost in antiquity.

Many populations believe that your eyes are the portals to your soul. Some believe that young children with their uncorrupted minds see strangers as they really are, friendly or fearful. Often in a VN hamlet, I could pick up an infant without a disturbance and be recognized as a friend because the small child accepted me. The psychology of this is important for the way military enters a particular population.

When I entered this village, a grandfather handed me the baby. If the baby didn't cry, I could be trusted in the village. I stayed two days.

My intelligence and psy-ops were always dependent on what the military was up to. Counterinsurgency deals with basic survival of family. Below is a picture of a grandfather in Danang, Vietnam building a school for his grandchildren in a refugee camp.

He knew more about psy-ops than the Pentagon or anyone else they could hire. He knew the insurgents and the personal cost to cooperate with us. Over the years, the Americans came and went before he could depend on them. In my two years, he knew who I was and that I had shown a favorable attitude toward the Vietnamese.

The subject material of this book (*The Headless Snake*), explains the experiences, qualifications, and resources utilized to program full operational missions to test deployments that created the Sheath, Spear, and Shield and the Peace Team Forward principles of Persuasion with Relevance as a strategy replacing other failed tactics. This strategy is flexible enough in design to be adaptable to most situations short of an initial main force battle. The time and point of entry are critical as to deployment of this strategy; it is not a tactic to be used to divert or submit a failed, overly aggressive tactic.

The current trend to utilize small strategic insertions or attacks to eliminate terrorists' leadership or to precipitate insurgency actions to change leadership or governments may not make our MSM (mainstream media) news. However, on the local front, it is counterproductive to finding any current stabilizing peaceful solution to military activity that doesn't produce "collateral damage" with loss of noncombatant lives, which is apparently everywhere our military goes.

Persuasion with Relevance has proven itself in limiting population and support resources for an insurgency and enemy during military operations. Whereas, Phoenix was an illegal and immoral counter-effective program that actually affirmed the Vietnamese local VC and the "shadow government" against the US mission. In my opinion, the CIA-Military Phoenix did, as directed by Colby, as much to defeat the Americans as any enemy element during the war. The program was fully aware that the psychological missions I developed were more successful than the "murder incorporated and torture" strategy prescribed by Colby and the CIA. Today a modified concept of Phoenix is being deployed as Special Operations and again will fail to advance any sustainable American cause.

The American military has the technology and manpower needed in today's world, political and economic environments, but has a serious lack of the necessary strategic leadership and direction. Instead of sending Special Operation Teams all over the world and building bases everywhere to threaten possible enemies, we should be screening all of our military for those who can also be trained as cadre for the Spear Team and Peace Team Forward Teams. Military training definitely has a place and need in today's world, but the military must recognize they are not the answer to all things. They must adopt a different image and as required a different performance. That's what this book is about, a strategy of assistance rather than dominance, one of empowerment to a better lifestyle.

When Congress failed to take corrective action against William Colby and the Phoenix Program after admitting before a committee that the 68,000 (+) Vietnamese civilians killed (murdered), most *might* have been guilty of opposing the government, this was the turning point that has led this nation down the path to becoming the world's greatest rogue nation, killing without respect for human life, based on deployments founded on lies. This government military policy of killing and torturing of suspects to enhance intelligence and after-action reports with emphasis on body counts has succeeded in destroying the basic principles of our Constitution and our Bill of Rights but produced not one victory. The very basis we have by treaty sworn to uphold in good faith in our foreign relations with all other nations has been destroyed by our military leadership. To attach our foreign policy to Israel by pledging to support the nation that has refused to comply with treaty and international law, killing anyone who opposes their criminal excesses, brings the question if our national policy is or is not immoral and violates international law by serving in our military while embracing Israel.

Are atrocities committed by Americans being reported in our wars as sensationalism to sell books? I doubt there is any real evidence as to much of these Vietnamese stories, as I can vouch for conduct up till 1969 in Vietnam when the CIA began its wholesale murderous assault on the Vietnamese people. Phoenix allowed the torture and murder without restraint by our military. As the legends of war build out of the fog of war, much reported about Phoenix and Chieu Hoi as "war" stories that were supposedly taking place during the time I had access to the operational plans and actions were legends, not in fact. I have read stories of Phoenix taking place 12 to 18 months before it became a reality. I have original records of my operations and assignments in my possession.

These authors, most of whom never saw the war with it in their faces or blood on their hands, could get the answers in interviews; they wanted to enhance their stories, if not the truth. All atrocities are bad; by definition they can be classified as uncivilized, that is to others rather than our military. I opposed this activity of Phoenix for a "black ops," murdering a young Vietnamese family and was removed from the mission by Colby after 22 months in country. My psychological operations and missions in the field were successful by encouraging mostly peaceful, nonviolent strategies with the indigenous population. We gained much better military intelligence and Chieu Hoi defectors with our system than Phoenix. You will find more about these books and stories of atrocities and legends of battlefield actions in other books. These books capitalize on the carnage of war and not on the interface of many good deeds performed by the Americans to help the Vietnamese. The bad things point directly back to bad leadership and officers.

Wake up America! It is not now a bipartisan political world war; it is the growing actions of a rogue government empowered by corruption and lies to benefit the few.

This book is my effort to sound an alarm that our war is not China, Russian, Iran, Syria, Iraq, Afghanistan, or defending Israel or Saudi Arabia. I can assure you if we continue to push our economic demands on the poorer countries we will be friendless and encourage them to unite against us. The methods we are using to attack other nations are savagely immoral and have never succeeded. I recognize that force against force is at times unavoidable, but it can be tempered to reduce the cost of post-operational settlements.

I charge our American military to turn to an introspective analysis of what they have become and take action to change. If not, they will become the losers and fail in their mission to provide security for Americans.

DECLARATION OF MY INTERESTS

In my research, one might say in search for solutions as to the current status of war and peace in the world, the much-touted COIN and its widely acclaimed impact on Iraq and Afghanistan wars appeared to be the most noted. As a reader, understand that all material enclosed is based on research of documents or in the field under conditions of war. As I have researched many books written about military operations and Phoenix that happened during my stay in Vietnam, much of these have taken literary license with the facts as I know them to be. In all of these tragedies of war there are legends, many without basis but are retold and circulated as facts.

I will state that a lot of activity went on but was always released with only the favorable positive side being exposed. More people claim Phoenix-ICEX as a participant operative because of its reputation as a CIA dirty tricks program murdering Vietnamese, and that was more exciting than their dull, assigned position to a sector. My credibility is well established by the documents included in the Credentials chapter. There are some stories printed that I know were not the facts. There has been considerable effort to rewrite Vietnam history about counterinsurgency programs (COIN) and Phoenix.

I repeat, my desire is to substantiate the truth as I experienced the war and to reverse the trend that has the United States Military and CIA invading other countries and indiscriminately destroying property and killing civilians not engaged in any conflict with the United States. All foreign intrusions must have a basis in fact, publicly listed, as to logic and reason to commit our peo-ple and wealth in support of such an invasion, as it is not the practice now. Failure to comply with this, the responsible parties should be held as criminals and prosecuted as such. This government has matched or exceeded anything the Japanese and Germans did in WWII to populations who we now just describe as "collateral damage." There is something wrong with the way we look at human life, as though it is a justifiable purpose to kill for political or economic advances; I might say totally uninvited. The visual memories of the after-action scenes on noncombatant civilian, women and children killed and savaged for no reason, by American army units still stirs my soul.

As an American, I do not feel the need to emphasize my allegiance to the American way supported by the Constitution as adopted by the founders of this Republic. I view all peoples as survivors, not as masters or as slaves; their heritage is as formed by place of birth with influence from environmental and habitat conditions more than spiritual or political factors. The necessity of opposing any efforts to unfairly restrict any survivor of their human rights as casualties of war or torture should be on the conscience of all humans.

Our spacecraft (earth) presents us with problems of survival that become more vital as our population expands to critical proportions. The management of our resources becomes ever more important and to suggest that accumulation of wealth by a few selected governments or peoples is an acceptable agenda breeds conflict. Along with greed comes the constant companion of the appeal for wars driven by and for economic gains that have produced war material capable of annihilating hundreds of millions of people without due cause. All for what? Gold, oil, food, water, power, or religious control?

This planet has limited resources available, to neglect this fact seems an absurd folly, and to fight over them as if they were property of one and not many is a bigger folly. I should note here that oil is still considered "black gold." The countries with the most militant histories are those with marketable oil.

The subject of this book is psychological operations. We have developed from Stone Age existence to space travel; why hasn't reconciliation and understanding not advanced from our tribal beginnings? To allow violent wars to justify the deaths of civilians (collateral casualties) as a justifiable aspect of wars is to declare human life has no value. And this must mean *theirs* and *yours*, a situation that in excess could mean the end of human civilization.

At different times and situations, I have worked with Iranians, Pakistani, Japanese, Chinese, Russians, Germans, and Vietnamese; all were deserving of my respect. So, I have a question: Why can't our Departments of State and Defense respect these people?

I take it for granted the CIA does not seem to get along with anybody but serve the elite and political elements of government.

My choice is to support the government and people who take the bigger view of the world than those who have off-shore bank accounts. When the choice of religion or the manner of government are the issues, they can no longer be maintained as having the only solutions as to who lives and who doesn't. Logic and common sense are the solutions to disputes, large and small, that can be developed by Persuasion with Relevance and Peace Team Forward. If the controlling force of these disputes is directed by greed or sectarian causes there will be no solutions, as we see in some conflicts today with perpetual wars.

From my experiences, I hold to the belief that these United States are so exposed to the world that protecting it from "terrorism" is impossible, and the millions spent trying to accomplish any efforts beyond the basic identification of suspects is a waste. Money would be best spent to bring our troops back home from 173 foreign bases and wars. Instead of drone bombers and surges, try a welcome wagon approach to win friends and influence people. Read *Peace Team Forward* in this book.

Persuasion with Relevance

This book of psychological operations is to support the development of trained military to function effectively and minimalize the tragedies of other conventional military type actions. It is not the intent of this author to defame individual members of the American military. It is to show how the differences in understanding the use of psychological operations have led to the failure of the COIN concept by the Pentagon. Can the Generals provide claim their years of war in the Middle East have been profitable to the human race? The tragic loss of life and property in these wars outside of the United States of America must lay on those who originate them: The President, Congress, and the "Military Industrial Complex," all for profit, politically or materially.

It is easy to anticipate that with world population growth, and as megacities increase in number, that "collateral damage" from any conventional war would produce deaths, not in thousands, but in hundreds of thousands. An attack on the infrastructure and population of these centers would have such a colossal impact as to disable a nation without ever engaging their conventional military.

It brings to mind the saying, "People who live in glass houses should not throw rocks."

That's right; I don't have all the answers. The world as it now functions is a complex mess that must find new solutions. We are all prisoners of geography and our heritage.

This book offers a method to reduce the waste of wealth as pursued by those who worship the art of war and those who are firmly established in our government.

Success starts in the training, the enumeration of specific cultural and tactical factors needed for each deployment. Create Team leadership from the selected personnel who have initiative and the ability to innovate to resolve problems.

The Team personnel is exercised as a group in training to develop coordination. And additional training as each individual is independently given field trials and tests to create self- confidence and crisis decision making.

Things that come up in training, these are just a few... "PTA" Planning, Training, Attitude. Planning the deployment strategy completely. Only those trained for the deployment permitted, no exceptions and a positive attitude toward the local population and their culture.

Team training will cover the development of fundamentals of local food and water resources and advanced first aid in order to quickly provide assistance.

Assume you are aware of the influence of color and that there are good and not so good colors that reflect mood. These color influences can vary from culture to culture. Know which is which before you get it wrong.

You must understand and observe the differences between matriarchal and patriarchal society. Know the culture's proper greetings and religious customs. After learning all the things their way, learn how to present yourself properly as to who and what you are, why you're there. If you select the right personnel they will really get involved with all of this...it is a *MUST* to be successful.

Most travelers want to take their home culture and lifestyle with them, especially the military; there must be a compromise with the local traditions...don't go native...be what you are without offending anyone. Look at the local culture as a place to learn and show interest. With a little time, you can, so to say, "round off some of their sharp edges" with improvements.

You cannot train a standard army unit in 90 days, never in two or four weeks; you need select individuals for these Teams. There is a lot of training before you engage the population, depending more on culture and habitat. I have never observed a military training manual on how to win and influence friends without poking a gun in their face.

In these poor countries, their house is their only sign of successful survival, often for several generations; treat it as your own. These search and secure sweeps by the military are the enemy's best psy-ops. *Persuasion with Relevance* has better methods.

Repeat, this is where the concept usually fails:

The incorrect selection of Team leaders, there are criteria to be met. The same as to Team members, there is also a necessary selection process with criteria.

I believe comingling tactics as COIN as deployed causes many problems and failures. The Sheath, Spear, and Shield were designed and tested to be adaptable for most situations as the strategy where applicable and not as a cover for other tactics. The one thing other tactics all have in common is the use of force with Psychological Operations, and all of these type actions are dominated by the presences of and use of the military, and if improperly deployed can be seriously counterproductive.

There is a lot to be done to install and develop the psychological approach into most military organizations. The first task is the selection and training of the proper personnel and the reorientation of command channels. With the proper training, these special Spear Teams can almost be universally deployed to any emergent situation, not just against an enemy.

Two factors we found as major deficiencies in our field tests with Americans were the ability to understand and use terrain (topography) to advantage and observations of environmental intelligence. We developed field training to improve upon these shortages.

As you have or will discover from this book, I focus the primary (and there are many secondary) problems on the military style of training. Conformity to specifications and directives just can't cover Psychological Operations involving indigenous populations with its current deployments. Instead, install my selection of personnel as a service-wide program and develop cadre for Psychological Operations (not the leaflet printing type) that can fulfill the requirements of leadership in a strategically developed operation (not a tactic).

You then can assemble Spear Teams and begin to retrain the Shield Units. As to the Sheath, there are essential intelligence aspects that need emphasizing and training. This is above the MOS current training.

The Military and Psy-Ops

There are general patterns to counterinsurgency, but it must relate to individual relationships as each is different and will fluctuate depending on a myriad unknown outside force. I can give you a personnel profile for the interfacing agent easily enough but finding the administrative and support personnel in a system over-burdened with staff and bureaucrats, that is a problem. To modify the way DOD, State, and the Agency function today is the bigger task. Counterinsurgency by its very nature requires them to act as part of a Team, jointly not individually, to the requirements of the interfacing agents; this is, in fact, reversing the chain of command. This game can be very dangerous and risky. I had the Team; we were not Gung Ho or Rambo. We did it for and by mutual trust; add *a bureaucrat* and you will fail, to fail means a total loss of confidence with the field agent. Failure means defeat and frequently death.

Integrity to fulfill commitments made in the field at all costs, the limits to promises must be made part of the planning. If failure to meet the security needs, with the basic element (element being the indigenous person or persons), to recover, the element must turn against the agent. In this case, the agent must eliminate the total element. We used propaganda to transfer blame for the elimination to the enemy. Failure is bad stuff; the Team must be "right."

As my work with military intelligence expanded and I began to deploy the APT as a blocking force in different main force assaults on enemy positions, my association with military and CIA operations became more involved.

The rocket attacks on Saigon became more frequent; the desire to stop them gained more interest. The CIA had intelligence that a North Vietnamese 122 mm rocket battalion with newer launching equipment was moving to attack the air base at Phan Rang. They wanted to capture the launching equipment. A top-secret attack plan was developed and deployment of forces was to start in two days.

This plan was to move one of the American's most experienced Regiments from their base camp to a two-day temporary bivouac in Phu Yen and be air-lifted to the air base and immediately into the assault. I had deployed 100 APT into a blocking position in support of the Regiment. This was a very important assault and was to start at 6AM just two days hence. The Regiment was already arriving at Phu Yen.

The CORDS Regional Director *(the bureaucrat)* called a staff meeting for the same day. The meeting turned out to be a briefing on how we as Americans should get to know the Vietnamese better; the bureaucrat had been in the country for less than 40 days and barely knew who I was other than the Chieu Hoi Director. We were instructed how to be American govern-ment representatives in Vietnam. How we never show our dirty laundry to anyone, show only successes. I was a briefer and everything I briefed was "good news;" Chieu Hoi was always included in the briefings. I had already been in the field getting the APTs into position for 24 hours and returned to Nha Trang for the staff meeting at 1 PM.

His opening: "This is important; I suggest you all take notes. I want you to spend one night a month in the field with the Vietnamese to learn about them. Here is a list; take pajamas, bathrobe, shaving supplies, deodorant, clean socks and underwear, and a flashlight."

At that point, an Army Captain came in and handed me a note from IFFV CG Rosson, "Meet J-1 and J-3 at helicopter port immediately." This was half of the IFFV General staff. I got up to leave with the Captain and *the bureaucrat* said, "Sit down; this is important. You cannot leave this very important meeting!"

I headed for the door as he was screaming at me to stop. I said, "The Commanding General is ordering me to report." He ordered me to sit down.

Well, I said, "I'm sorry. I must go, and if you come anywhere within a mile of me with a flashlight in Vietnam, you are crazy."

I could not tell him why I was leaving; if he had security clearances he would have known of the operation It was a crucial operation; this particular NVA unit was equipped with sophisticated missile launching equipment not seen in South Vietnam before. We wanted to capture some of it. What *the bureaucrat* did not know was that with the IFFV, CIA, and selected Vietnamese, (my Armed Propaganda Teams), I had already positioned them in the field that morning. I was to be part of the prisoner control and CIA interrogation team in the field during the assault operation. We were to attack a 122mm rocket NVA Battalion moving in to attack Phang Rang Air Base. It was a major, critical operation.

In the helicopter with the two Generals, they said the Regiment refused to break bivouac and enter the assault. We were going to relieve their General of his command and get the regiment moving. My job was to get the troops in trucks and to the airstrip. At Phu Yen, I was present when they issued the orders relieving him of command and the J-3 took over. I was getting the troops into trucks. They had no idea who this civilian was giving orders or where they were going but they responded quickly to my commands. Never knew why.

I think I was present at all of this as a witness third party to the situation and conditions of the Regiment.

The whole operation fell apart, and the NVA disappeared.

Washington political appointees seldom bring solutions, but they keep coming to build careers.

I was later in an Air America twin-engine Apache with *the bureaucrat* on our way to Pleiku and the engines began to ice up and the pilot wanted to return to Nha Trang. *The bureaucrat* demanded and was yelling at the pilot to proceed to Pleiku Air Base; he had a very important meeting. He had to be there. Now I knew CORDS never had really important meetings. Here we are, losing one engine, over the mountains, with no instruments and these big military transports popping out of clouds all around us. *The bureaucrat* screaming about his important meeting. I asked the pilot if the plane had two parachutes. The pilot said none, pointed to the carb temp gauges, the right engine tachometer. I could see that the carburetor was in danger of freezing; the pilot wanted to return to Nha Trang. I nodded; he put it in a dive and headed for Nha Trang. I was blamed for not supporting *the bureaucrat*.

About a week later I was at MACV HDQ Saigon, passed by this Major, a famous staff officer, (author of the Pacification, "Oil Slick Theory"). He asked how the new Regional Director was doing. I said, "He is a little incom-petent in some areas." I admit, a bad choice of words. Before I could get out of the building an all points alert was out for me to return to Region II, now! I was scheduled to meet with defectors over on the Cambodia Vietnam bor-der and did not get to Region II for two days. I caught hell and was deported out of Region II. Everything that was wrong in Region II became my fault.

A Regional Chieu Hoi Center was started before I came to Vietnam; the thing could not get traction because of the Vietnamese. I could not jump start construction without Vietnamese cooperation. I went to one meeting with them; the construction bids were rigged and excessive, the site was on a river-bed subject to flood, and there was no potable water source. I had managed a water and sewer district and was a general contractor in Texas, as well as a Mayor and Judge. I wrote one memo for distribution about the meeting, then I became the cause of the failure, as per *the bureaucrat*.

The bureaucrat was writing up my performances as a very bad employee; he didn't know that his secretary always gave me a copy of his reports. But this time they decided to reassign me to the Embassy in Saigon. I didn't know it at the time and not till recently learned the Major and *the bureaucrat* were Colby people. A field officer has little defense against the chain of command's bureaucratic code of survival.

When Tet '68 hit the Embassy, we watched from the roof of our hotel, the Regina on Pasture next to the SF billet in Saigon. I went into the Embassy after most of the shooting stopped around the building, went up to the 5th floor, CIA offices. There were only two men there of the staff; they said, "Answer this phone," then went to the radio room down the hall. The phone rang, "Hello, this is Embassy."

"This is Rostow. I want to know why the press hasn't gotten the report of 35,000 enemy dead."

"Sir, you need to talk to someone else. Right now, we don't know where Westmoreland or Bunker are. Hold on."

I went to get one of the men. Two days later I was told to get a body count, military photographer pictures, any way I could count enemy dead country-wide. There never were 35,000 enemy dead in the first 10 days; a lot of South Vietnamese were killed. In the field, there is nothing more depressing than actually seeing 5,000 poor, hapless noncombat Vietnamese civilians killed just because they were in the wrong place at the wrong time.

There is also the case of the Vietnamese airborne ranger school at Kontum; if there were any rackets, prostitution, black market, etc., these rangers had a piece of the action. They were the elite military units and rather independent. If there was intelligence developing, they had it. So, if in the area, some of us would go by for a jump with the class in training. It was just one way to identify with them and it paid big dividends. When the civilian type, non-military heard about it, an order came down forbidding us to jump. I can't say if we stopped.

When General Rosson put me in charge it was to consolidate the system, and avail to the military my influence on the Vietnamese government side and my knowledge in the field of the entire Region II and IFFV. Overall, all the men in psychological units were very capable and devoted to the psycho-logical operational deployment necessary in the country. They needed encouragement and someone to settle disagreements and issues. Like the case of overruling a Division Commander General's psychological plan to deploy four million leaflets in his territory to intimidate the population with threats.

There was the situation involving one of the officers, a Major, who worked for me in our Psychological Operations in the field. He was an Academy graduate, hardworking, seriously dedicated to our work. His rotation of six months was up and he was to rotate to a combat unit.

He wanted the 82nd ABN; we sent him up there to get an assignment. He returned and said he was rejected by the other Academy graduates because his time in Psychological Operations was a waste of time. I had taken him places the whole damn 82nd ABN Division (my former division) could not go as we were working on defections of units NVA and VC. On a per capita ratio, we were 20 times more effective than the 82nd ABN. On hearing this story, I went to IFFV HDQ to see the General. Sure enough, his door was guarded by an Academy Graduate Major; he said I could not see the General if I didn't have an appointment. I said I had one and pushed him out of my way. He went backward over his desk and became entangled in a secretary chair on wheels. The harder he tried to get up the more he became entangled; other than a loss of dignity he was unharmed. I saw the General and explained my aggravation to him. He said it was wrong but it was an Academy tradition of doing things.

A few weeks later another division had cornered a VC unit that had taken 40 students as hostages into a VC tunnel complex. The division was setting charges to bury all those in the tunnel. The division psy-ops officer, in order to save the children, went into the tunnel to negotiate and was killed. His Sergeant went into the tunnel to recover his body and was seriously wounded and the Captain's psy-ops unit nominated him for a Silver Star. Several months later I heard it was reduced to a Bronze Star by "General Review."

The division collapsed the tunnel, killing 40 elementary students and two teachers Why? I have only to guess that they counted them dead and enemy killed. After stunts like this our good intelligence sources and Vietnamese contacts just dried up in the area.

After I found out about the reduction to Bronze Star, I went back to the IFFV Headquarters to see the General; fortunately, the Aids had learned not to get in my way. I asked the General why the reduction. The Answer was that three Generals vote on awards and Silver takes all three, Bronze takes two; he would not give me the names of the three Generals.

For the last 45 years, it has been my opinion that the three Academies be moved and changed into OCS schools and stop this Academy legacy practice. The recent failures of our military only strengthen my opinion. There are good Academy graduates, but they are good as officers from their personal abilities, not because of the Academy or its legacies. I think it is best to earn commissions from more time in the field with experienced trainers rather than in a classroom. In Vietnam, generally the best and most reliable person-nel at battalion and lower were the NONCOMS with multiple tours in country and not officers.

Psychological missions in the field in support of a deployment requires officers who have more than warfare experience or training, but a firm understanding working with psychological tactics. They need personal people skills typically not found in most people because those skills are not needed in our urban society. *Not everyone can develop them.* The services need to start screening for personnel who have the skills and start advancing their training for Psychological Operations planning.

The wars we are seeing now directed by the Pentagon are absurdly stupid and whether on purpose or by design are counter-effective. It is more than a disgrace; it is a waste of wealth and blood of the Americans and those who have supported these deployments that kill and destroy countries for no known humane reason be held accountable for their gross neglect.

FRONT

LEAFLET NUMBER: 245N-81-68 AMOUNT: 100,000 REQUESTOR: 1st Cav.
THEME: Losses suffered.
TARGET: 95th NVA Regt.
REASON FOR DEVELOPMENT: To exploit losses suffered by 95th NVA Regt.

HÃY THEO NHỮNG CHỈ DẪN SAU ĐÂY ĐỂ TRỞ VỀ VỚI CHÍNH NGHĨA QUỐC GIA

Bạn có thể đến trình diện với 1 viên chức hay 1 đồn bót Chính Phủ Việt Nam Cộng Hòa. Bạn cũng có thể liên lạc với binh sĩ Chính Phủ Việt Nam Cộng Hòa hay đồng minh. Họ sẽ sẵn sàng đón tiếp bạn.

Trong mọi trường hợp, vì lý do an ninh, bạn nên theo những chỉ dẫn sau đây:
1. Giấu vũ khí một chỗ - Ra trình diện, sau sẽ dẫn binh sĩ Chính Phủ Việt Nam Cộng Hòa trở lại chỗ giấu để lãnh thưởng.
2. Khi đến trình diện một đơn vị hay một viên chức có vũ trang, nên đến ban ngày, và nên giơ tay lên để tỏ thiện chí của bạn - Nếu có giấy thông hành của Chính Phủ hay truyền đơn, hãy xuất trình.
3. Dầu không có truyền đơn bạn vẫn có thể ra trình diện. Khi đến trình diện chỉ cần đưa hai tay cao lên để giúp binh sĩ Chính Phủ Việt Nam Cộng Hòa và Đồng Minh hiểu rõ ý muốn trở về chính nghĩa của bạn.

Follow these instructions to return to the National Just Cause.

You may report to any GVN official at any GVN outpost. Or, you may come in to GVN or Allied soldiers; they will readily welcome you.

In any case, follow these instructions for security reasons:

1. Hide your weapons. Later you can lead RVNAF soldiers to the weapons and receive your reward.

2. When reporting to any unit or official whom you can expect to be armed, report only in the daytime; you should hold up your hands to show your good will and display a safe conduct pass or any other leaflet if you have one.

3. Even if you do not have a leaflet, you still can rally. When you come to report, all you have to do is just hold both hands upright to help the GVN and Allied troops understand that you intend to return to the Just Cause.

Leaflet produced by South Vietnamese government instructing how to surrender to Chieu Hoi.

CÁC BẠN TRONG TRUNG ĐOÀN 95B CHÚ Ý!

Các bạn đang sống xa nhà, đang mệt mỏi, thiếu thực phẩm cũng như thuốc men.

Các bạn đã từ miền Bắc xâm nhập vào đây để gây chiến và đã có đánh bại chúng tôi trong ngày 17 tháng 9 vừa qua nhưng các bạn đã nếm mùi thất bại, chúng tôi đã thắng và còn đánh bại các bạn nữa trong những ngày tới. Tại sao cấp chỉ huy của các bạn vẫn khăng khăng duy trì cái trò ngu xuẩn này?

Hãy ngừng gây chiến. Hãy tham gia với chúng tôi và sống trong hòa bình. Ra đầu thú và trở về với chính nghĩa. Chính phủ sẽ tiếp đón nồng hậu và bảo trợ chu đáo cho các bạn. Các bạn cũng sẽ được cung cấp thực phẩm và thuốc men. Chắc chắn các bạn sẽ được sống hạnh phúc cả về tinh thần lẫn thể xác.

2451-81-68

```
Attention: Members of 95B Regiment.

You are a long way from your home.

Your are tired and do not have much food and medical supplies.

You came from North Vietnam to make war. You tried to defeat us on
September 17, but you failed. We defeated you and will defeat you again.

Why do your leaders insist on this foolish task?

Stop making war.

Join with us and live in peace.

Rally and return to the right cause. You will be warmly welcomed, and
sheltered carefully b the government. Food and medical supplies will
be supplied.

You will surely be happy in both body and spirit.
```

    Psychological missions are more than leaflet drops. It is the combination of strategy, the directed use of firepower and targeting. Rather than "surge," a deploying of logistics as a tactic to avoid building a sense within the enemy of hate. In other words, the more you assault their population, the more they resist.

There are ways for civilian special ops to work with the military and vice versa, but it all needs to be worked on for future use.

Vietnam War was a failure in my opinion from several directions:

- It was a war that was politically based on American viewpoints and not Vietnamese.
- We underestimated the determination of the Vietnamese.
- The company grade American officers were poorly trained and lacked leadership ability.
- Too many bureaucrats came to enhance their government careers with their solutions for the war dreamed up in Washington.
- Murdering thousands of civilians to show progress by body counts was totally counterproductive.
- The American Military concept of war via total aggressive dominance was a bad strategy to begin with.

INTERROGATION LEADS

There were thousands of interrogation reports on POWs and Chieu Hoi in the Vietnamese system that were not reviewed or followed up as to good prospects for further inquiry. After initial interrogation, they just disappeared into POW or Chieu Hoi compounds. By following, especially Chieu Hoi, with family members (remember, family is the basic social structure in most Third World populations), I had more than enough intelligence to keep me busy without torture. I used Chieu Hoi APT to do the follow-up with family contact with me, never military. If I were in an area in the field I would search these files for prospects. I don't think anybody else was doing a careful follow-up. Everybody thought "Battle Field" intelligence was most valuable; it would be, but seldom did it pan out.

I especially centered on those Chieu Hoi and POWs with high school or higher education, business connected, age 25 to 45 with family, and any injured to follow up with family as a courtesy if they were accessible. I always came up with a good score of intelligence on enemy organization or an arms cache; the information was turned over to Vietnamese commanders of the compounds and a delayed report follow up through MACV channels. This way I protected the security of the informer and his family. If reported through American channels, the compounds would have been over-run by Americans causing chaos. My interpreter always thought it funny that we could get good intelligence after some of his classmates from interpreter training class didn't from the same informants working for the American Army.

You will read more about Third World nationals and their different cultures; family is the building block of their societies.

The defector program was the most important element of Psychological Operations; it was in itself a difficult program for the enemy to attack with their psy-ops.

We also developed another interesting intelligence source. When we knew of a military sweep of an area where suspects were picked up for interrogation, they were held in a "holding pen" until they could be sorted out as to those of interest. My Team would watch those held in the pen and from our experience with "body language" identify the NVA and VC officers who, when interrogated, would be sent to POW compounds. We would send an APT member into the compound and offer them the choice of becoming a Chieu Hoi and indicate my presence outside of the compound.

This always worked; they preferred Chieu Hoi over POW and the military interrogation. We scored very good intelligence. We did not report these methods or we would have been over-run with all those who wanted credit for our success and would have screwed up a good thing. Again, understanding the situation as it influenced the suspect and not the military way of conformity and uniformity. We learned.

Presence in meeting with enemy suspects and the ability to determine the leaders provided my Teams with good suspects for interrogation, and me not in military uniform. I appeared to be just one of the Vietnamese interrogation Chieu Hoi Team, and we immediately began to build his status within our group.

No torture or physical threats We established a position of status with the subject and did not degrade him.

Torture is a sadistic deformity of the character of the interrogator who uses it.

PSYCHOLOGICALLY THINKING

This is the result of a struggle by the author to define psychological operations with its current successes and failures as compared to the original methods and strategies developed by the military in the Vietnam War. In this process, I have reviewed 30,000 pages of reports, letters, blog sites, news coverage of all types, books, and sources, and my own files developed during the Vietnam War.

War in itself is a huge subject coming from history and current events around the world; there seems to be an epidemic of causes. One must assume that it is a human trait to be possessive and belligerent about one thing or another. Some situations require more or less aggression than others to settle disagreements, but some can become more about their doing "war" rather than just dealing with the cause of the disagreements.

I compare psychology to "air we breathe;" it is always there but not often noticed or how we deal with the methodology of it when it comes to using logic, reasoning, and common sense as a strategy in warfare. Psychology is the essence of our actions. Without thought and methodology, there can be no reasoning and no logic. The mind has to be informed in order to be responsive. It takes unique skills to observe and categorize your contact; you breathe in making contact with the enemy or insurgent for the first time. All the while, he is doing the same.

This is the moment of truth.

Since General Petraeus produced the Counter-Insurgency Field Manual, I have been wondering how I could have successfully completed 30 field operations in Vietnam without having a manual, report, or a COIN Center to tell me what and how to operate in areas influenced or controlled by the enemy. But our military is struggling to deploy in Afghanistan with all the support the concept has attracted; it is still failing.

THE AIR WE BREATHE: We use this terminology to indicate close contact is necessary.

I think our military fails because we attempt to practice global psychiatry (Note, we can't even cure ourselves) instead of using psychology. We should be using a reasonable methodology based on our analysis of the psychology of our opponents.

The difference is the "air you breathe." It is not what comes out of your manuals and classrooms concocted by people who only think they knew the air the Taliban (in Vietnam the VC and NVA) breathe. Their survival has given them a strength that is something you don't read about or find an expert to lecture you about. I learned from my subjects, and just by coincidence none had ever been to Harvard or worked for Rand.

We are at war in a tough environment that has a history of wars and of corrupt central government; the population is more tribal based than homogenous as one. Afghanistan is the crossroads between mega-countries but has never been given the opportunity to advance their lifestyle because of so many conflicts over control. The Americans with their Allies have invaded for no apparent reason that justifies our occupancy of a foreign country.

Add to all that, in order to justify our aggression in Iraq and Afghanistan by the restyling of an old tactic to a new and wonderful concept "COIN;" a creation based upon revitalization of "psy-ops" claiming to support an "unconventional warfare" of less violence. But it was not correctly deployed and was used as a tactic to support Search and Destroy or control. It should have been a strategy to find less violent solutions where possible.

Begin to reduce all this COIN data to an acceptable size textbook; there are some very good points to take advantage of to improve the training of individual personnel to advance the Persuasion with Relevance as the strategy.

Redesign the unit concept to a workable version of the Spear Team.

Set the parameters for deployment into an operational format. (This is where the new meets the old head on).

Create a new leadership classification for Spear Teams and begin recruiting Armed Forces wide for these specially qualified individuals. Set up a training regimen on "the air we breathe," environmental intelligence recognition, and "people skills," plus an introduction to sustaining the necessities of human life under all conditions.

I state that Persuasion with Relevance is an option available to fit the circumstances as a strategy; it is Psychological Operations. It is our best security and defense of our country by aiding and supporting the survivors of the world with good intentions. (As opposed to plundering and forcing our standards as theirs unwillingly).

I can correctly assume that I am an unknown in this world of elitists and patronages, but I am content with that status because of the air I breathe.

Apparently, this country has involved itself with China which brings a warning from me that the new leadership is very "tight" (my Chinese friends used that word and I think they meant "old fashioned and determined" as a change in attitude). My people skills have taken me through Vietnam and Vietnamese, China and Chinese, and Japan and Japanese, as open societies for me. Whereas Europe to me is old America, Asia is new and different, more dynamic and interesting.

HOW DO I EARN YOUR TRUST?

One of the first obstacles encountered in psychological operations in the field with the local population is to establish trust. Due to the wide range of conditions, each situation must be studied in detail and determined what can be influenced, providing the most relief to the population. Security is important, but it must be organized to include the local population and not be too domineering or restricting of their activities as a community.

A major self-help project involving local population working alongside the military.

In our field operations, we found that being alert and organized but not forceful, always working with the local population, produced a favorable environment to start with.

A MEASURE OF YOUR SUCCESS

If you are doing your job properly with Psychological Operations and in close contact with your subjects, these type events will come naturally and often. The conduct of you and your Team is constantly being observed and analyzed by others as to your performance. If you are living up to your promises and showing a positive attitude in working with them, they will respond with support and cooperation.

When the population starts coming to you for help and begins to help you with your endeavors, you are on the right track.

Psychological operations are strategies used to create an attitude that is beneficial to the population and can provide freedom from suppression and resolve grievances. The message must fit the situation and be practical enough to accomplish what is promised. Any efforts to reform must originate on their side of an issue by them leading the changes beneficial for them. Incorporate your Team into theirs, instead of theirs into yours.

The chapter "Events" are only a sample of the more unusual circumstances that were brought about by doing something right; none were solicited.

What was amazing about these "Events" was how far a reputation can spread among the indigenous population.

In looking for hamlets and villages to do field operations in areas that no one had programmed, we were several times met with villagers who were knowledgeable of some of our activities and openly desired cooperation. A point to make: we were mostly working in areas of the country where there had been very little or no government activity. Also, we found some discrepancies in reports of security where an area was reported secure in the Hamlet Security MACV report that had not seen any government, Vietnamese or American, patrols in six to eight months, but had been treated to several VC psy-ops propaganda sessions in recent weeks. The content of these VC sessions gave us a basis and opportunity to refute their propaganda. In 1966 and 1967 the VC psy-ops was very poor, and mostly about unification, but by 1968 they had really improved their message. The Cuban Bay of Pigs was always described as a big failure of the US to overthrow a communist govern-ment, pictures of the anti-war marches in the US, and they brought racial issues up as how blacks were mistreated and forced to fight in Vietnam.

Persuasion with Relevance: Properly developed and made a part of the strategy and properly deployed as a means of eliminating or reducing the violence of war.

The aftermath of American Search and Destroy, Hunter Killing Teams, and Drone Bombers as applied in Iraq and Afghanistan will never be healed, damage money and lies cannot cure.

RECAP:

- Deploy early; melt into the local environment and cultural pattern as much as possible. Don't go native; keep your presence of what you represent.

- Each phase, each population, must be carefully planned and organized as a separate campaign. It is not the answer to all problems, where it is applicable there are definite advantages
- Do not adopt the image of a military armed suppression of the population. Remember the keys to this concept and follow them.
- The Shield has a definite part in the deployment and can contribute to the successes. The personnel are military oriented and can be structured to meet many different requirements, not only security (the primary responsibility) but improvements that add to the population-environment.
- Our government is in control of careerists responding to bureaucrats making all changes difficult.
- By your education you have been instructed; now it is time to learn.
- There are no two living things, if you have not observed it, alike on earth; genetics sees to that.
- One "black ops" can destroy years of work establishing workable relationships.
- Be natural, be yourself; happiness is the great motivator. It is contagious; be positive.
- Contingency, always.

Refugee housing for displaced families who were forced to flee their homes in active combat areas.

CHAPTER 3

PEACE TEAM FORWARD

The objective is to develop a deployment of military trained personnel that has a dual role, one in military service and one as cadre for civilian disaster relief teams. The Spear and Shield Teams are to be used to penetrate enemy perimeter territory to establish security if there is questionable enemy environment. To attack large base areas of the enemy is not a good strategy, whereas it usually involves unnecessary civilian deaths. Draw them out to protect their resource base, and alert them and their support with Psychological Operations with the promise of safety and defection awards.

Note, even the larger urban sites are not self-sufficient enough to survive on their own resources for very long. *Attack their logistics and personnel support carefully.*

Forty-eight years ago in Vietnam, I worked all this strategy and details out in the Chieu Hoi and Phoenix field operations. What I learned in the field was there are many ways to accomplish something. One was the "military way" and the other was Persuasion with Relevance with Peace Team Forward. The transitioning to Peace Team Forward was conceived in war and successfully tested against a formidable enemy (one that eventually defeated the American military). My Teams were all trained military, former VC and NVA processed out of the Chieu Hoi APT Vietnamese program, which was actually a psychological military operation. Before I left the country, there were 7,000 APT members available. Six times I posted up to 150 APT members as blocking forces for American military operations. I had installed within the APT program additional training programs, out of public view training in presence, intelligence, squad level light infantry, developing self-help hamlet programs, and how to work with US military scouts when necessary.

A training field trip to Lac Doung District to practice the technique of face-to-face contact with APTs.

Experience in the field was a great teacher.

Based upon experience in the field face-to-face with the enemy is "the air we breathe." We found our Persuasion with Relevance Teams were much more effective when properly utilized than the typical military units as they are trained, with the appearance of the Teams being more civilian in appearance, dressed in plain clothing identified as *Peace Team Forward* and unarmed. In missions where security could be a threat, the Teams were lightly armed. The Shield Team was available on call nearby. The presence of the Teams this way was received, and the indigenous population interrelated easily with them. The Shield Team as a reserve defense force was kept separate from the population and remained separate even after they became accustomed to the presence of the Team armed and in uniforms outside of the populations' daily activity. The objective is to be less in appearance of a military invader and more of an interest in protecting the populace.

Yes, good operational intelligence must be established, and we had the methods to produce it; it's not in a Field Manual. It goes with the success of the Teams; locals will keep you informed if you are accepted by the popula-tion. And this takes training in Psychological Operations and good leadership.

As for civic action, we found that projects started as self-help fared much better than any other. The project supervision must be local and recognized as a leader, directly involved in planning of any activity.

These areas where security has been established by the Persuasion with Relevance Teams shift into Peace Team Forward phase and a more stabilized environment of government controls which allows the Peace Team Forward to expand and upgrade self-help projects, all while the Spear Team moves into new territory.

Yes, it is not this simple. It takes timing, as before you start blowing up birthday parties and funerals, etc. Teams must be trained with the right personnel. Our successes generated even more successes, and word of our deployments in the hamlets and villages spread out; we were often met with welcomes.

To test our approach as to methods, we skipped from one province to another, miles apart. We avoided any chance of a fight in any village; that would prove nothing. However, in our travels, we did get involved with a couple of VC "arrow patrols." These patrols were fit to fight and were responsible for deaths of many American military who were poorly trained in how to counter them. Establishing a base of fire on a patrol in rough territory is not the answer.

TRANSITION TO DIFFERENT DEPLOYMENT OBJECTIVES

I would like to see, as a starting place, the conversion of two divisions to the Peace Team Forward organization concept. Peace Team Forward was created to advance Psychological Operations favoring the indigenous people with less or no violence. I want to stress from the beginning this transition of the primary military mission, one of a predominate military mission to a dual mission concept utilizing the Persuasion with Relevance method. These divisions would maintain their basic military structure as trained and organized for action as it were as "Good Samaritan" (aka Peace Team Forward), a person who helps another or others in need unselfishly.

In the many daily missions in the field for the Chieu Hoi program and the 30 psychological field operations against the enemy foe, it became clear that uniforms and guns displayed on strangers were not well received by the indigenous population. The "Team" designation is to further reduce their reference to militarily related identities as much as possible when deployed in their nonmilitary missions.

The uniform is emblematic of the military as to wars and all that goes with wars.

We identified our Team members as non-military and we were in the process of putting **PEACE TEAM FORWARD** on the typical Vietnamese (APT) clothing in Vietnamese and English to down-play as much as possible any observable military presence or dominance. We were operating in unsecure and enemy territory. The clothing that the Teams wear is not a military uniform, but it has a psychological point; no nation name, no rank, no standard color; the only identification is printed on the front in bold letters...**PEACE TEAM FORWARD,** so the indigenous population gets a frontal view, giving them a view of your face.

We avoided nation's name so they will ask, and open face makes a better connection between people. They will learn it is the United States; we want them to figure it out. The overall image is to appear like a work force of different trades on the ground working...not a dominating force.

In our psychological field operations, we were using our strategy of Persuasion with Relevance rather than Search and Destroy, a typical military maneuver in securing and holding contested territory and the indigenous population. We successfully utilized the Spear and Shield Teams as our entrance into contested territories We also found "How can we earn your trust?" was much more effective aligning up the people than "Winning hearts and minds," in translation one asks for their permission and the other indicates a change. The Peace Team Forward was our operational unit after security in position was obtained and we began advancing "self-help" projects.

As for the gathering of intelligence, we found that body language skills were very important and in their Vietnamese hamlets as commune style living they often knew things they didn't know were of intelligence value to our operations. In entering these hamlets and rural communes "presence" was needed and could be the difference between success and failure of the mission or possible confrontational combat on first meetings. In the first contact, we always asked permission if we stayed overnight.

This strategy will pay more dividends than you can dream with all positive results.

DEMILITARIZED NAVAL AIRCRAFT CARRIERS CONVERTED TO OPERATIONAL CONTROL AND LOGISTICS BASES FOR PEACE TEAM FORWARD

I had completed work writing *The Headless Snake* and had started to draft an outline of a deployment order (five paragraph field order). However, there are so many options and varied conditions, I looked for a simpler solution.

Peace Team Forward is a movable municipality with a fully trained and experienced staff, fully equipped to meet the requirements of providing the essentials for survival under extreme conditions for material and human damages from natural causes or war.

I began to survey for an example or model as a possible deployment field order as a solution. Then I remembered from my Naval Reserve time being on an aircraft carrier, and it was a floating city. I found five carriers parked out of service at Norfolk Naval Yard, made to order, just sitting there going to waste.

Demilitarize a couple of them, paint them white and you have your *Peace Team Forward* operational base, a sustainable floating city as a base and supply facility and operational nerve center. These carriers can be converted with construction equipment and very few modifications, some additions of engineering construction equipment with a complement of Army Engineer Battalions and Seabees as a start, out of military uniforms and in the Peace Team Forward attire in the deployment. All other features that come standard as designed with these carriers can sustain up to a 6,000-member crew.

And it is amazing how complete the carriers are to be the ideal emblem of peace without their aircraft and to fulfill the needs of the disaster recovery, hospital ship, and logistic support, etc. All while promoting the Americans in a profile of *peace.*

Within these carriers, some have had a personnel force of up to 6,500 including 2,000 as ship's crew as an estimate. The 4,500 combat personnel can be replaced by the dual-trained Peace Team as described military predesignated Army Engineers and Navy Sea Bees as the basic complement, as a situation may warrant other peace oriented industrial sources of personnel and materials, with area of flight deck available for nonmilitary use for storage of materials and equipment, with deck area for helicopters.

The carriers are equipped to respond, once set up for Peace Team Forward, to where ever help is needed. All systems ready to deploy at a mo-ment's notice worldwide. It becomes an operations center equipped to serve as an aircraft control base, a hospital, housing, materials storage with equip-ment, along with a highly trained cadre stationed on board with additional personnel as needed, drawn from the military divisions and bases that have had the dual training or in positions as trained for Peace Team Forward. Then there is the ship's crew who can assist with the deployment once on station. Addition of units like "Doctors without Borders" and "Dentist Smile Teams," and the possibility of other disaster trained groups can be added.

Facts:

- One benefit, the use of idle equipment strictly for peaceful use, as a beneficial portrait of America: *Peace*
- Second benefit, personnel duly trained with career, potentially higher quality and more involved, with higher morale. Building a stronger military potential with the alternate occupations.
- Third benefit, this is not expensive. You are not capitalizing the cost of the carrier; most of the equipment needed for Peace Team Forward deployment is already in service and not in use. Operational costs are much less than maintaining other overseas interests.
- Fourth benefit, this is a gift; "We need to change our image in a world that is getting smaller day by day from a militaristic

domineering corrupted government transitioning to become your good neighbor"- Uncle Sam

- Fifth benefit, returning the United States to a Constitutional Government. The facts from history, wars are expensive in every way; they provide no benefits, whereas properly organized free enterprise is much better all around.

I would put an auditorium in part of the hanger area to show movies of the ship, its capabilities, etc., in severe disasters as an instructional media on survival.

Land locked countries should be offered transportation to the carrier on tours to see what "Uncle Sam" is up to in the world. Just remember everything that touches this ship is for Psychological Operations, peaceful assistance, and not psychological warfare.

This concept is a part of my push for the military transitioning to meet new and changing world conditions.

Think about it; after all the killing, bombing, and destroyed property, the final result rests with what the people do to reinstate their lives. I have to wonder; we recently sent 1200 American troops to the Philippines. I assume this move was to threaten China. This was shortly after a disastrous typhoon had killed 700 people and destroyed several villages. Wouldn't it have been better to get a hospital ship and relief supplies there first with some engineers or Seabees rather than Special Forces with guns? You know the destruction is unnecessary, but the cost of it generates enormous quick profits for the "military industrial complex." It is a fact that those profits come from wars which produce nothing of value; they are destructive of earth, of which we only have one, being irreplaceable.

Something our bankers and "elite corporations" won't tell is how far they have corrupted our legislation and military; you can see for yourself their dis-regard for human life.

The reason I am promoting transitioning our military is to protect our Constitutional government, our economy, based on individual effort rather than government entitlements, and society based on the Four Freedoms. Freedom of speech, freedom of worship, freedom from want, and freedom from fear. We should be preventing the international corporations of criminal fanatics profiteering from the New World Order. They have abused our military defensive capability; it is there to protect our country, and it is not their blood and property destroyed for their desires. From past experiences in private industry, I know it is a fact that international business works better if functioning openly and freely in an assured peaceful environment and with-out our Special Operations teams positioned in their territory. Teams who are hidden somewhere in their home, country or their businesses being tapped by American spies.

So, we have as Americans, no choice but to change how our military is used and how it can be used peacefully to return our government as our Constitution ordains how, and where the military functions, and remain a strong force as needed in defense.

This is not a cry for disarmament; it is a request to find new and better strategies.

PROPOSED IMPROVEMENT OF ENLISTMENTS

Look closely at another advantage of Peace Team Forward personnel. There are multiple ways to benefit. After the military (I emphasize military) has completed basic and advanced training, then we need to teach the trades and skills that are necessary to build (reconstruct) all aspects required to exist; shelter, water, waste water disposal, food and food preparation, electrical, medical, transportation, roads etc. For those who are obligated to a military career, regular service, they can then contract for Peace Team Forward for 20 (+ 10) years' service to obtain training in one or more of the necessary trades. In most cases, obtain a civilian license if future employment would be desired. Over time, Peace Team Forward personnel could build up the reserve forces with military technical trades available when and if needed. As well as their military, MOS would be available from the dual training. We would be building a professional, career-oriented military. This strategy is not to disarm, but to capitalize on the use of personnel to benefit their careers for standing ready to defend our country and support our Good Samaritan efforts.

This, I would say, should reduce the *desertion* rate and the *suicide* rate by creating a society-immersed, para-military existence along with active reserve comingling in training and community activity, an exposure to daily associations. The possible addition to various training of trades could add re-medial education classes, if it becomes necessary, and add foreign languages.

Building character, skills of real soldiering, leadership and useful skills and trades...all with *good will traveling around the world*, if no disasters, etc., make friendly ports of call for Uncle Sam to be seen supporting *peace*. Remember the whole time the ship is active; personnel is being trained with the opportunity to work with other foreign personnel, (rather than possibility of bombing them). If those in the military have never labored closely with citizens of other countries, shoulder to shoulder where both take pride in the work, you don't understand human nature or how to win and influence friends. Which I think is obvious as observed of the current status of our mil-itary.

Success of this deployment concept depends upon the integrity of command; that is, to demand no CIA or any sp-ops to be directly involved with Peace Team Forward. You cannot mix the two; Peace Team Forward does not need their assistance. I personally don't trust them or their motivation, due to our current status in the terrorist's perpetual war keeping the world unbalanced.

Peace Team Forward is not a direct participant in war; it should have an advisory board overseeing its performance and development. Its dual trained military personnel could be reassigned as needed in critical war time and in peace working as Peace Team Forward creating friends and allies. (note: This is not a USAID concept; it is above their capacity and ability).

Ship security can be applied as required with deployment, a "police force" for onboard and standard military security screen, escort naval and air if needed but not made a big issue. Suggest and arrange UN security of disaster area deployments. And in some situations, use the carriers as training space for countries we consider true ally quality, living up to our standards of humanity.

The ships' complement will be skilled and advanced in urban necessity trades and skills. It is a psychological mission for **Peace Team Forward**; make no mistake, it is not a deployment of special ops or CIA criminals. **PERIOD.**

It is essential to recognize that the Third World countries do not have the alternatives that industrialized countries have today as they are brought into the global wars incited by a few criminal governments for control and greed. Their strategy appears to put no value on other human lives (Gaza-Syria) and deploy our bombers and killer teams against others, murdering and torturing as many as possible. Their excuse being it is to install a democracy for all the people of the world by the USA, the remaining super power of the world post WWII. *The national security strategy of the United States of America* as directed by the President is the authority used to invade selected countries. (While elite corporations exploit the countries' resources, at the same time fighting terrorism obliterates their country and people).

It appears that our American military and CIA organize, support, and direct much of this murdering for profit. Like it says "the buck stops here," as with the military "chain of command."

Not only who, but what gives the American military the authority to engage in these wars? Don't the generals have the intelligence to know these small countries are dependent on the family-based society as the family members are essential to survival? When our military kills children, we are destroying family and society, and they have no alternatives than to rely on and align with countries to destroy America. When we are dealing with these limited resourced populations, a different tactic must be utilized to interface with them as friend, not enemy.

We did not go to aid the Vietnamese; we went as invaders and exploiters. And we lost, losing 60,000 of our servicemen and four million South Vietnamese. It now appears in that war committing over 500,000 of our military, we didn't learn anything; the lessons have been ignored. We have not won a war since WWII but lost thousands of men and trillions of dollars. Can anyone elicit for me the benefits from these last 60 years of our military?

Yes, I am unknown, and I have researched every day since 9/11 the military; the more I searched, the more I found to search. The book, *The Head-less Snake*, the strategy, *Persuasion with Relevance*, and *Peace Team Forward* are the results America needs to transition its military to a helping hand rather than using their gun hand as the only strategy for war, not peace. I seek no notoriety. I want to see a military transition to a humanitarian interest in strategy along with its typical defensive posture at home. I do not want to disarm our military. I want to develop it so the manpower can be used effectively supporting *peace* as well as defense.

We are at a place in time to exercise our desire for peaceful humanitarian life through the elimination of pain and suffering for profit and power. Think, maybe the gun is not the only methodology to obtain our national security!

The continuing murder of the helpless has evolved as:

Sacrifice the few for the betterment of the many.

To kill and destroy the civilian populations is made justifiable because their military needs the civilian support. They, too, can be considered as enemy.

Torture is an acceptable means of gathering intelligence on the "enemy" because we are Americans and the New World Order Super Power.

Is this symbolic of what Americans want?

AN OPEN MESSAGE TO THE MILITARY

This is a communication I had never thought I would write, but times and situations do change. I thought I would publish the book and be done with it along with the 30,000 pages of research into nine years of government military publications and contacts within the active military of late and all the files from my VN office sent to my home address in 1968. I cannot let the book, *The Headless Snake*, as currently written, when published, be my last voice about the "methods of war" deployed by the United States military. History more than sufficiently exposes our inadequacy, not only of military force, but of the nature of the environment and societal structure of the supposed enemy. You failed to assimilate your strategy to reduce the potential carnage of your attack, a mistake that has been excessively costly in human lives and property.

These Third World countries survive as close to death as any peoples; their society is based on family structure and for most of them their only asset, a continuation of the basic pillar of life is family. The loss of any member of the family threatens the whole family. With a possible current estimate of up to eight civilians to one of enemy in war you can never claim victory, only perhaps a massacre.

Now if you are old enough to dress yourself you are old enough understand the purpose of my book, which is to transform how our military operates in the world. It has never been my desire to single out individuals to hold responsible for the failures of our deployments or the failure to develop an adequate security of America. Traditional methods, some are only wasting lives and wealth, making situations worse. That appears to be the objective of warfare, not security but profits.

I am experienced and knowledgeable of your craft, and if you continue on as you have been plodding along and resist necessary change; there are others who are interested in the concept. And since it is for peace I find no fault in that, as Peace Team Forward does not conflict with our freedom. It can be safely adapted by other countries.

These next pages will provide a little deeper insight into my abilities and experiences. As well as criticism, I offer solutions, field tested successfully in war from the point of contact up to the command level. Not all wars are of the same cause but of the basic point of contact; they are all generally similar. After 50 years post-Vietnam, the military is still confused how Psychological Operations are best deployed.

Face the fact; if our security was our military's primary objective you would approach Israel differently by having Israel comply with treaties, inter-national law, and open to inspections, via the UN. Otherwise, until this is accomplished, our insecurity that Israel represents is just one of many other risks our military is negative in resolving for political reasons; or does the military have an authentic logic why you risk blood and wealth?

My read of our Constitution provides for the military to act independently to protect our borders, borders that are now open and unprotected. Yet you have troops stationed all over the world, protecting what? Our borders, from whom and how?

Over the years I have had associations and friends in the Far East as a result of time spent in Vietnam; in the past, I had PLA (People's Liberation Army) contacts with senior military officers without problems as my friends. It is an understatement to say most Americans do not understand Asians, and actually, the government classified them as "subhuman" even during the Vietnam War. Well, this gets more attention as the "air we breathe," how we relate to other races, their cultures, and environment.

Will the Pentagon ever learn that being the world's primary super military power does not always mean being the most successful at whatever they attempt? In fact, it fails to list a single victory in the last 60 years. Having the best relationships can be more powerful than any other means.

The renewed recent attacks in Iraq and Afghanistan have ignored the psychological impact on the Third World populations. The US military does its best to be the best invader, air assault destroyer and family killer in the world as their universal tactic (save and except the CIA's mercenary murders). What Petraeus did was not Psychological Operations as I would describe it and de-veloped with the Sheath, Spear and Shield concept. My strategy was defi-nitely less noise and less visibility and more working with peripheries to eliminate enemy support and gather intelligence. With the intelligence, keep moving in and around the principle leadership of the insurgents. The strategy of Persuasion with Relevance was developed without American military participation in the field except for logistic support from Special Forces. (Ladd and Kelley were good friends). Our field work was successful and started our concept to penetrate and spread in advance of our arrival in villages via the Chieu Hoi APT Teams returning from association and training with us.

The most difficult opposition I encountered in the process of deploying this concept was our bureaucratized military staff supported by careerist employees (military personnel). It was a constant problem and was why I worked the Vietnamese side to avoid it; especially since our security in the field was at times vapor thin.

The so-called shadow government was the Vietnamese government by 1968. I found from experience the less USAID or MACV personnel involved, the better, other than those who might have been involved and knew better than to trust with deployment information. Being a member of the IFFV General Staff, I was able to coordinate to avoid conflicts and having access to COMUSMACV report auditing section and the unaudited field reports and my own intelligence agent net source; we managed very well. My intelligence net covered the whole country, and I was the only American to use the agents I worked with; all were within plain view. No one ever caught on to my net and for their safety, I could not reveal who they were. I picked up on them via the "air we breathe."

Persuasion with Relevance pretty well describes the concept, matching effort to environment and society. Primary effort to adapt to indigenous population needs and beliefs by not looking and acting like the military that is destroying their lives. Caution: don't go native, have presence as an American.

For America, a brighter, peaceful future will come by developing different military strategies from those carried over from WWII and Vietnam, the ones that gave the military the idea of being the only world Super Power. (I might invite you to meet friends in China). Then there is the White House with *The National Security Strategy of the United States of America 2006*. Summary of it is the justification to attack and kill in the name of Americans for democracy the world over. Peace Team Forward is a concept that provides all positive features that can as a military transition resolve most, if not all, of your organizational problems.

Now I could write another book about the Pentagon problems from a different direction because of my experience in military aerospace development and manufacturing on how to control contract expenses and actually audit the contractor's books. Washing out all the fluff. It may not be obvious to those without experience in industrial military complex that the "tail wagging the dog" is the industrial military complex and not security. I assure you it is, and it can be corrected.

Peace Team Forward was developed during the Vietnam War; it is a military concept and is not a public group or bunch of peace-minded activists demonstrating against the military. The Peace Team Forward and Persuasion with Relevance strategy will have a strong military foundation but a modification of mission and deployment and in large part a modified image. Persuasion with Relevance is, you might say, the "assault" phase if deployed into an area in stress from violence. The positioning of the Spear Team and Shield Team versed in non-violent methodology of war is vital. The Teams are specially trained in addition to their MOS as Psychological Operations. When security is established the Peace Team Forward assumes the operational responsibility emphasizing "self- help" projects and de-emphasize all impressions of military actions.

I support the transition of two infantry divisions as a start of mobilizing the dual qualifying of personnel for Peace Team Forward units. These units will begin training in Psychological Operations and the development of skills determined necessary for what is typically referred to "Emergency Relief Operations." Rather than constantly repeating their MOS as infantry, they will also be trained as engineers, electricians, and other utilities of the skills required to answer to emergency situations on a stand-by position. As you explore this concept you will find enlistments improve as to qualification, a real boost in active reserves as this spreads into the reserves with those who have these skills and occupations. If you openly accept this concept you will have the opportunity to influence more peoples and countries than you ever could with invasions or surges.

I caution you that you will find opposition from the industrial military complex because the profit margins for Peace Team Forward equipment are less than those they steal from war material.

Advantages of this concept:
- Reduction in the need for foreign deployments.
- A more stable and higher quality of personnel.

- A much greater support from the public.
- A balanced military budget.
- Stronger relationships and treaties with key foreign countries.

The dual configuration of divisions does not weaken your offensive security capability. It will increase the active reserves as their training will provide civilian career opportunities.

The following promotes how you and this nation's military could impact the entire world without firing a shot.

Surprise, Surprise, Surprise

General, get on your phone; call Russia, China, Iran, Israel, and NATO! Announce that the United States of America, civilian and military, invites you to join us in our deployment of 3,000 personnel, equipment, and materials as our first **Peace Team Forward** mission to clean up and restore Gaza to a livable condition, organized under the direction of the international court.

We come unarmed and out of military uniforms. We have asked the UN to supply and support all security measures as necessary. The announcement of this will be supplied worldwide and a leaflet drop in surrounding countries. Be advised that any threats or fanaticism against the deployment will not be tolerated for a second. The response will be instantaneous.

It is time we start shaping this world for our own and let us determine it, not criminals or fanatics.

We will set up a communication's center in Gaza and invite your input. We will initially utilize the military only for logistical and communications support.

We hope this will be one of many in the future as we become more organized.

There is a future alternative to this described for a more advanced solution of *Peace Team Forward*.

CHAPTER 4

TRANSITION

Implies: a passing from one condition, form, stage, activity to another

I was asked why I waited 45 years since Vietnam to write about my experience in Vietnam, and my answer was simple. I thought my government was so conceived to protect my liberty and freedom, but since 9/11, I have become aware that it is not.

Then came the wars in Iraq and Afghanistan and being more than a little knowledgeable of military strategy and tactics I began to read because I sensed something was wrong and unethical about this government. I read and researched more; it became obvious my government had become totally corrupted. We have been illegally spying for years on the whole world with NSA (military operation) and have secret operations in more than a hundred countries. After discovering all my records and files from my work in the Vietnam War, I had a base to work from that no one else had to make comparisons; it was time to go public. I had hoped the military would stand its ground and protect the Constitution in order to peacefully prevent a rebellion. However, the military, due to lack of good leadership and too much incompetence, has failed, as Iraq and Afghanistan plainly show. Maybe this book will stir some interest, and we can work to restore the Constitution and the Bill of Rights. And then the proper presence of the military will encourage the American population to take back their government and clean the corrup-tion out of all parts of the three branches of government. Thus, the book *The Headless Snake,* based on experience and not on interviews. Hell, it is my country and worth the try.

The American military must be advised to transform. Why the military? Because it is the only element that is a self-sufficient, sustainable part of the government and the largest. We start the transition in part by leaving behind their dysfunctional historical traditions and strategies by starting from the bottom-up and top-down in order to meet today's challenges. The transition-ing must begin in finding less disastrous strategies, tactics, and deployments, with less emphasis on violent force and military dominance of the non-combatant civilian population. Why change military strategies? Because big wars have the technical potential to be so devastating that millions could perish in seconds if attacked. Small wars are completely worthless. A waste of life, wealth, and time spent that could be dealt with negotiated settlements if it were not for the international arms dealers (industrial military complex) and those who purposefully agitate populations over government, finance, and/or religions, etc. to keep the world unsettled. The American military is one of the primary agitators serving unknown interests. A brief mention of the Joint Special Operations Command (JSOC) and US Special Operations Command (SOCOM), they could be considered as a new development in changing our military, but they are retreads that have been glamorized to be expanded while the rest of the armed services are suffering cut backs and RIFs as a result of budget cuts. (In the future, we will hear more about these secretive forces and their legality, which is questionable).

The military keeps adjusting itself, as one strategy fails they change the name, creating a new and better strategy but have yet to make any serious changes to their concepts of fighting a winning war. Yes, the War Colleges and Think Tanks have been busy producing concepts to replace or improve COIN in exquisite detail; for nine years (2008-2017) I have been reading thousands of pages of theory, concepts, tactics, and military history and strategies. I found that to explain "common sense" they took 200 (+/-) pages. All very enlightening but fails to recognize that the military is not the Peace Corps, nor can they represent themselves as a functioning government as anything more than military advisors. And still represented by uniforms, guns, and, most often not, to be denied security of their operational bases.

Then there is the "Peacekeeping & Stability Operations Institute (PKSOI) paper, "Hearts and Minds: A Strategy of Conciliation, Coercion, or Commitment?". Based on this paper I began to wonder if I was ever in Vietnam, but as it happens I am one of the very few senior MG (CORDS) ranked Americans left alive of the 1966-1968 period when programs were being implemented into the most active period of the war. "Wining Hearts and Minds" sounds good but "How Can I Earn Your Trust" worked much better. As for the record, General Westmoreland did not lose the war; his tour in the war was very successful subject to conditions. William Colby of CORDS/CIA and his Phoenix Program contributed more to the loss by realigning many of the South Vietnamese people (who were in support of the South Vietnamese government) against the American invaders.

In Vietnam against the VC, NVA, and their Chinese (PLA) political warfare officers, I developed methods to deny their forces in many operational areas. Their control of indigenous populations was a source of what the military called - "infrastructure" and later as "insurgency," and finally as "suspects." There was also a classification of the enemy known as the "shadow govern-ment;" which, in fact, included some of the Vietnamese civilian population, including those working for the Vietnamese and American governments.

I am a realist and believe that as a nation we must always first make our lives as best suited for our environment and our heritage governed only by our American Constitution (not by Executive Orders), and by cooperating only with other treaty countries that respect the inalienable rights of their people with peaceful intent. Until further notice our nation is based upon the sound principles formulated into our Constitution and Bill of Rights that guarantees our freedom and liberty; it is ours to keep or lose. Those guarantees are in serious jeopardy as our military is sliding more toward becoming an enforcement tool of the Executive Branch of the government, which is a violation of the Constitution.

I am a believer in people. I don't see them as foreigners or strangers but as survivors, just people; just like us (not as subhuman as we labeled Asians after December 7, 1941, and the Vietnamese as to the reason why we never registered their graves during the war). Some populations live with the advantages of favorable location and their heritage, while others live under difficult conditions of nature and some from the burden of adverse political conditions. All of these factors influence and create a system of constant change that has the potential to produce conflicts that are agitated and unsettled by aggressive police and military responses. Guns and uniforms are the traditional military signs of force and dominance that are often visualized as signs of danger. We must create a new image of our military breaking away from traditional use of uniforms and other tell-tale signs of past aggressions. Strength can be displayed by means other than bayonets or guns, and the showing of compassion is a greater sign of concern and strength than aggression. It is time for a change and storage of some of the impeding military traditions.

How to start the necessary military transformation: that is the question. We must encourage the military to adapt a military force that reflects courage and compassion versus power, dominance, and wealth in excess. There needs to be more emphasis on planning and alignment with our basic national concept of freedom and liberty. Though I am of the opinion that the military personnel needs enlightened as to just why they serve, I do not place the blame for failure directly on them. This transitioning will require a huge effort and some fundamental changes in leadership and strategy. If started as soon as possible with the internal cooperation of current officers and staff, I will show how to train and organize them on how to avoid some of the recently failed deployments, a new alternate strategy for unconventional war. The "military" will have a much better feeling about their careers in the service of their

country. (Military active duty is telling me morale is now very low). With new organizational planning, it can avoid some of the current RIF (reduction in force) and work toward a reorganization of units and training that will greatly increase the utility and confidence of the military.

Our work space is limited, looking at it as a space ship (earth) that confronts the world's population with endless problems of habitat, resources, and weather, to name a few; and our ship has many problems. It will not increase in size but our population will. Should we be more interested in solving political problems (war) or deal with problems of nature such as feed-ing the population? Then there is the property damage of earthquakes, hur-ricanes, and volcanoes. We must realize our solutions will deal with all of these, plus human behaviors of a very diverse population. We must recognize that no two countries are alike, and due to environment and location of each there will never be a way to determine parity, the difference in wealth of each. So, each must be considered individually, peacefully and legally.

Before we forget, we recognize that all people are different as it is. It is due to genetics that no two living things ever on our earth were, or are now, exactly alike; resulting in an endless variety of problems that have no one solution that fits all problems: This is inclusive of the military's dominance and/or aggression. However, I have never viewed a military budget that gave serious attention to nonviolent resources or tactics that produced real efforts for peace.

This brings us to the question of supporting survival; the weak versus the strong, the poor, less fortunate versus the fortunate, and due to technological advancements, the intelligent industrious versus the limited, and finally to the conformist versus the nonconformist. No where do we find that one race, religion, or nation can claim a superior position above all others. I do not support the New World Order or any other such plan; it is not only impractical but immoral. To control such a situation, the masses of people would have to be marginalized by reducing them to little or no more value than as disposable slaves for the elite.

The American transition starting point is with the military, where we must act in compliance with our American Constitution as to our objectives to develop and equip a military force within the prescribed limits of its utiliza-tion. I have not been able to find the current standards to which the American military is required to live by; their use of torture should pretty well convince you they have no standard or knowledge of the Declaration of Independence.

As long as there has been a profit made and a nation willing to pay, war has had the option to be whatever standard that is needed to be deployed, and it appears more for profits from war than for security.

This brings a divergence of missions, of cause and effect, that has resulted in the tragic loss of life and wealth with no appreciable benefits for our population or any population. Our government and military function as if there were no Constitution or Bill of Rights restricting their activities. From Vietnam to today, our military has engaged and lost every known deployment overseas, costing thousands of American lives, millions of foreign lives, and nothing to show for it but an oversized industrial military complex. This includes an inflated cost due to total mismanagement, and without question, the lack of competent planning or leadership. Our position as the world's leading government is fading rapidly.

Before we consider possible strategies, we must have a realistic military mission statement, one based on what the military's manpower requirements are to meet the responsibilities of the Department of Defense; under whose directives and whose oversight? And more specifically, what are the imposed limitations? When this is provided, we must then set the size and organizational pattern of personnel and equipment with the costs to meet these various mission requirements.

The Annual White House National Security Strategy Report, those that I have read are a general declaration of war based on a false premise of estab-lishing universal world democracy by the world's Super Power. Like it or not, the USA will insist. Especially if there is a profit to be made for the military industrial complex elite corporations; then we will attack.

It appears that Special Operations Teams are currently being reorganized to defend our sovereignty worldwide. I really have a difficult time figuring this out. We put military teams in three quarters of the world's countries but leave our borders open and undefended. Our Constitution and treaties prevent the military from operating outside of public view, deploying only when the sovereignty of the USA is threatened, and a response is approved by Congress. The sustainment, stability, or any other involvement or otherwise connection with any other country should be considered illegal unless is obli-gated by treaty. The military has no authority to deploy teams into countries to advance conditions for just any reason or for private corporations. Each team deployed must be covered by treaty, publicly approved by vote of Congress. Make note that our Special Operations teams reportedly deployed in 100 countries (+/-) are protecting our perimeter providing security for the homeland; amazing, just amazing.

The defense of our country and the expense of this defense will not create wealth for our country but to a high degree is an obvious necessity relative to the enemies we are now constantly creating. If we can agree on the direction our missions take us, we then are in a position to determine what challenges we must be prepared to deal with militarily when approved by Congress.

- The active defense of our nation's borders and our sovereignty by supporting a free people from attack, from without and from within, if invaded.
- Meet our treaty commitments and review all such to maintain our obligations subject to world conditions.
- Be ready and able to protect our sovereignty in battle primarily at home from all foreign threats. Support emergency response civic action at home and for our allies (Spear Team, Peace Team Forward as a function of *Persuasion with Relevance*).

Now that we have a beginning doctrine to work from, we can look at the impact of the transitioning and realignment of the military around different strategies and concepts of military power, as adjusted by time and world conditions. The use of which will be controlled by Congressional vote, publicly taken in open session.

The debate has been about the alignment of military forces to serve principally in the COIN configuration and the slighting of the conventional main force alignment as an irresponsible decision. The COIN concept has shown the signs of failure as it has been deployed. A main force alignment concept would indicate that we anticipate a confrontation with another super power on a battle field or theater wise. Under the circumstances in the political and economic world today, this would be unwise and technically it would be foolish.

The defense of our nation's borders: The short answer is we can only do it to a very limited degree. The new rocket powered ship-to-shore or ship-to-ship missiles launched with inertia or photo guidance at Mach 5 plus speeds with a range in excess of 250 miles may become the weapon of choice We can't jam or catch it; there is no real-time defense for it. Now consider the economic geography of most of the industrial countries which have located most population, industry, and commerce on their coast line. How many of our primary defense installations and nuclear plants are less than 300 miles from our shore lines? If we have drone intercontinental bombers, who has a drone sub? Most industrialized nations are vulnerable to attack from sea without an invasion. Defense is best served by making friends rather than enemies, which appears to be counter to our current military command and political desires. They talk it but appear to lack an understanding anything other than conventional force. This alone should encourage the development of the Peace Team Forward forces. (The demilitarized air craft carriers modified for Peace Team Forward are potentially a greater force for stability and economic liaisons than a drone).

Between oil, petrol dollars, and Israel we are in for a future of consider-able stress. We must bring our military back to the States, if not only econom-ics but also as homeland security (not a police force). And for transitioning, in part, to a more effective use of personnel and materials, plus retraining.

In theory, apply some logic to this requirement of homeland defense; what does the United States have of value looking forward 50 to 100 years that needs to be defended? A government system, the population, and industry? We have a land mass with a natural transportation system via rivers and valleys, two ocean fronts, railroad, coal, oil and farm land. Why attack us to destroy us? Take out the grid; close five or six ports and either starve or freeze most of us to death or just destroy our currency for the same effect, all currently possible. Something to think about, this would not require a super power enemy to accomplish. Offense is the best defense, but instead of allowing a corrupted cabal directing our military, let's do it the old

American way involving the citizens toward the support making friends; a helping hand has always been more successful than a gun in hand. If you don't know how to do this, I will show you how...I have had practice (Persuasion with Relevance). On the larger scale, reestablish America as a center of trade and manufacturing rather than the world's war material and armament dealer.

Emergency response civic actions, why don't we act like a good neighbor and react to these natural disasters around the world with enthusiasm as Peace Team Forward? I recently read an article on Afghanistan which stated we had to destroy it to make is safe; 2,000 or more homes were destroyed. I have studied the design of a concrete modular shelter, truck transportable sections; if it had been introduced in to Iraq and Afghanistan it would have put them to work promoting "family pride," better living conditions at less than 20% of the cost to maintaining our military, and this project is manageable, corruption free. And is more favorably remembered that the dust of a Hellfire missile. The benefit from this would be you still get your oil pipe line at much less expense and with safety. Although I assume the Taliban has been teaching our military a thing or two about defending their homeland. Have we ever tried teaching them anything constructive? Of course, there is our support of a corrupt central government and profit from the opium; what is the cost in human lives for this? Who gets the profits?

There is no debate to this; if we had used Psychological Operations and properly developed it, we would not be the world's most hated nation and peoples. All thanks to our military and political misadventures and lack of foresight.

Yes, I think COIN was never advisable, as deployed was a disaster, a military mistake; and the fact that it had swept through the Armed Forces so completely must bring tears of joy to the eyes of our enemies.

Persuasion with Relevance for this book has been simplified, but the Spear Teams are built around selected qualified experienced people of the military; it is a military strategy (non-conventional) but can impact a society if the peaceful assistance is used when initial contact is possible. The dual trained military personnel units deployed as a component of American peace rather than NATO or Israel.

Success is in the selection and training and not in a Field Manual. The Shield is a deployed conventional military force, like all deployments, comprised and equipped for their task. (I have to say it; some of the officers I risked life with in Vietnam were the best, but this was a minority. Most were incompetent and were freely allowed to glamorize their reporting. From what I have read and been told this has not been changed at all levels). I am not sure the military fairly represents the true nature of Americans deployed in foreign countries.

There is no depleting of conventional military forces with this strategy. The Spear Team functions best as deployed with a ratio up to five or more indigenous personnel when possible to one properly trained American. The Shield is a conventional force sized for the mission.

The Vietnamese defection program (Chieu Hoi) was very successful and part of Psychological Operations. It was established but had lost its integrity due to corruption. If I did one thing in Vietnam, it was to straighten the Psychological Operations Program out and give it direction, until the CIA totally corrupted the integrity of the program. I personally worked with four CIA officers from the four regions. Three of the four officers were very capable and good men to work with.

How to persuade the military that the Spear Team leadership as trained for Persuasion with Relevance is a strategy and, in the process, producing leaders skilled in innovation, motivation, adaptability, and resourcefulness? (This will be discussed further). The CIA is a separate case and must be brought under command and control, and not allowed to go freelance.

A quick reply, "We lose wars because of the lack of good officers and comingling the missions with civilians (political appointees (USAID) and military (non-career academy) personnel within a pyramidal structured management." Of course, the missions do have to have a basis to begin with. I would hope. But I am not sure we haven't attacked or invaded based on conjecture or purely for political or economic gain and not for security. How many civilian lives have we murdered? Why?

My people skills have gotten me into and through a lot of things. Experience is a good teacher; it makes you think beyond conformity and uniformity as instructed.

I don't know if the military wants help; they have learned that people have short memories, and failures can be made to look like successes with a little PR. With the current status of government corruption as it is the generals will have to react or accept the responsibility for our immoral behavior.

This book, based on research and experience, is a simplified approach to Psychological Operations as Sheath, Spear, and Shield basics; as to command structure, simple, you tell them, you do what you are told to do by the Spear Team leader, period. (You don't need an FM for that).

I have added some credentials and personal data and the Events chapter to illustrate the scope of my work and experience.

Chapter 2 covered the selection techniques of personnel, especially Spear Team members; and the training of all Team members with the essentials of advancing strategy, planning, and deployment in detail, either as a force or as a counter force so as to develop an exceptional cadre to show the world it is investing in *peace*. And they will be schooled on how to properly interrogate suspects and POWs without any use of torture or abuse. Torture is another subject, and I have information and advice from APA in exchange for my considerable exposure to it as it was involved with interrogations. I perfected techniques that were very successful in Vietnam with the use of environment rather than pain.

Since the US military may be content with high body counts and losing wars, and not open to experienced help I might as well have to give this away and spend the last years immersing myself in other things. There is nothing classified in my writing.

I had hoped to promote Psychological Operations to the Pentagon as the world is possibility faced with a world depression bordering on the Dark Ages. All the industrialized nations are facing failing economies and can be faced with riots, small wars, insurgencies and conflicts that could be better served with fewer surges and Hunter Killer Operations and drones; served better with more Persuasion with Relevance utilizing Spear Teams and Peace Team Forward.

I stand on the fact that war is by its nature a struggle between aggressors, each deployed to defeat the other. Winners and losers may be determined only as a point of view of one or the other participants.

Victory or defeat can be judged in terms of economics, gains of resources or territory, a political shift in government, or by military superiority. Is it worth the cost?

It would appear in Afghanistan that the winner will be determined by the degree of political control that is influenced by one participant or other. And to this point, neither participant is winning support of the majority of the population; one due to a corrupt central government, and the other from the military aggressiveness as an invader. Who benefits from the opium trade? It seems that the push for total military superiority by one participant over the other has alienated the general population support for either.

I can see how the intrusion into these wars by the United States as to the methods employed could by the recipients of our attacks consider them as crimes against humanity. In fact, they are and approved by our government.

There is something terribly wrong with the circumstances, politically and economically, being created by the United States recently over the last 60 or more years in particular.

For instance, step back and take a second look at the Departments of State and Defense; both have been engaged in expanding our hegemony by economic and military dominance that has not been beneficial to this country, but quite the opposite. As observed, it has been to a selected few corporations.

I saw as of 3/8/2011 in *Defense News* that the military is in the process of realigning its deployments and budgets. And I would make the point that 21st century warfare has long passed trench or blitz-krieg strategies and now must recognize economic strategies as well as forms of unconventional warfare. Since Vietnam, the participants must devote attention to worldwide TV coverage influencing public opinion for their actions.

LET US PUT IT ALL OUT ON THE TABLE

The United States has a large, some say huge, military that actually produces no wealth for this nation; and in fact, the entire military budget is an expense and as of this date has been unaudited. It is a tax on the people. The military claims it is necessary to protect the country from terrorists. Save tell me, how does destroying Libya, Kuwait, Iraq, Syria, and Afghanistan, along with killing thousands of civilians in these small countries, protect us?

Military action:

Why is there so much pressure to destroy to make it safe; primarily using little or no direct human forces to obtain an objective? (Operation Drones) If we are to desire a negotiated solution or the capability to put in place our requirements on the population after we have destroyed it, what have we accomplished? Are we trained to kill and destroy indigenous people because we think they are a direct threat to our citizens or just because they are of no value to us the invaders? I assume there are some slick answers to these questions. The most popular is that we will rebuild and advance you into a better, more productive lifestyle, the one we choose for you. Would you like our American solution, "The Iraq" version?

Their next question may be then *why are your armies here killing us?* Because it is more profitable than just training and marching in parades in the States. From a study of WWII, the rank promotions came faster to those in units taking the highest causalities, and in peace time it is due to new units or reorganization that opens up promotions, such as COIN and attacking more countries to accelerate promotions.

There was so much the military has claimed as results from doing things the COIN way. Is that why we are failing; what after 12 years fighting a light infantry force? Just when did we prove the Taliban crossed our borders?

As I am closing this section there could not be a better story to make my point than the one about the gunning down of seven or eight Afghan boys by American helicopters. This single event will set back every psychological effort to win over the indigenous population's support that has been made to date or future.

AGAIN! As I stress in my Persuasion with Relevance that functions around and under the total command of a military experienced Team Leader, these leaders are specially selected for people skills and trained in Psychological Operations. I could be the least known veteran of Vietnam because my work was best if not made public. I don't need to read about Psychological Operations (psy-ops) or about insurgency warfare, because I was there developing operations. Learning by tests of different methods and techniques in a war five times larger than and just as ugly as Afghanistan; working against a well-trained North Vietnamese Army with Chinese advisors and their political warfare officers. What I now see from Afghanistan is not success, but failure.

Viewed from experience, the career advancement system of our military has been defined by combat actions by quantity and less by quality. You could say the noisier the action the better, and the higher the body count the better; career enhancement. Our military needs to be re-educated as to 21st century means, methods, and requirements, but not to slight power and force measures, but emphasize dual capability and a more career professional military personnel. Learn which wars to fight and how to fight them to win. Our military could be reduced to something slightly better than a national police force based on its 65 years of military failures. Due to the complexity of the populations and terrain of the world, you cannot control the whole thing; try making America better instead!

If we want to control oil why do we keep making costly mistakes over and over again?

IS CHANGE POSSIBLE?

As I have continued to research and strain to make sense out of what I read from a wide variety of media and government sources, I sometimes sit back and let my mind wander to shift swiftly through the exposure. I hear the religious right claiming it will all be just fine because it is God's plan, what will be is meant to be and it is best. And I hear the liberal and government socialistic propaganda and then the New World Order schemes pushing their lies that are a total contradiction and in opposition to my leanings of freedom.

So, what to think? The American military must change in order to meet today's challenges and restrain these criminals, those who created the trans-formation of our government to rule by elitist power over the military. Our military must transition to a degree of independence that defends the true law of Constitutional government. They must start to find less disastrous strategies, tactics, and deployments because these are one of the primary tools the "elite" use to keep our country perpetually at war. There are those who relish world power and control of all wealth and freedoms of all peoples on earth. It has been our Constitutional government that has been a formidable obstacle in their progress, and now they have nearly subverted our entire governmental system.

There are those who are situated in positions of command in our military and now appear to be manipulated by criminals who have diluted the capacity of our armed forces to deploy and sustain a favorable solution. One that advances peace while preserving moral and humanitarian relationships. One that builds nations rather than rape and steals their resources as profits for the elitists.

Wake up Generals, or are you just a careerist or a peacock with no real grit? What is your mission in life, to follow or lead?

Having served as a General Staff Office in war and in command of missions in the field (VN), I understand some of the pressure on officers, and I now question what appears to be questionable leadership. I gave blood 16 times at "dust offs" in Vietnam in 22 months, but I will be damned if I would salute the North Vietnamese Military as the most senior officer in our American army recently did.

I enjoyed my tour in the 82nd ABN. As an officer in Special Troops with the three ABN Regiments kept intact, we got a lot of odd assignments. I had six days date of rank on the Academy class that year which put me top of the list. A few of the odd assignments: One, I was the awards reader for "posthumous awards" from WWII Silver and Bronze Medals. My God, what these men accomplished, plus sacrificed their lives for it. I must have read 100 awards, only once was there family in attendance. If you were at Bragg, this took place back of Main Post Chapel in the grassy area with a flag honor guard, a Colonel and me. In Vietnam, I was authorized to endorse awards and was rating my officers. (I don't think you want to hear my opinion about that).

When the Communists blocked Berlin, the 18th ABN Corps code officer's mother-in-law was on the wrong side of the fence, so he lost his security clearances. They sorted personnel with holes in cards. They ran a wire through for a new code officer; I was the only one in Bragg qualified. I inherited the AFSAM 7 codes and machine. During the temporary time I had it to meet Corps requirements, I was cleared for every sort of clearance. No armed weapons were allowed on base except for MP, Pay Masters, and Code Officer.

Special Forces was forming at Smoke Bomb Hill and their first Adjutant was from the 44th TK; I was jump mastering for a lot of their night jumps, mostly my manifest did not speak English. I was offered an early Regular Commission as Captain to go SF, but they were being sent to Japan without dependents. I deferred. (I would have brought Jump Master status, communications and code experience; would have brought Top Secret security clearances and trained as an Armor Officer...all skills they urgently needed). Also, the Egyptians offered me a commission and the officers there were paid more than the Americans, as well as being offered cotton futures.

I could be interested in approaching Peoples Republic of China and Pakistan; both governments are in the process of dealing with insurgent populations. Not to give them any advantages, but to interface them to establish trust, but only with government approval. I have worked with both in the past. Actually, some were in the classes I attended at Fort Knox.

CHAPTER 5

PHOENIX-ICEX

THE STORY BEHIND "THE HEADLESS SNAKE"

It all began with a briefing about the strategy to be used in attacking the insurgency, which was originally called infrastructure. The infrastructure, it was supposed to be members of the general population who were supplying the VC with various materials and food to support their tunnel complexes. The geniuses running this war ignored the fact that they did not understand the complex nature of the Vietnamese population. To know and recognize exactly what the mindset was as I refer to as the "air we breathe;" meaning you had to live it to comprehend it, and it was not available from lectures or books. It was nearly impossible to learn if you were in a military uniform carrying a gun, seen by many Vietnamese as a foreign invader.

At this point in time, Westmoreland was being blamed for the failure of his strategies to defeat the Viet Cong (VC) in the field of battle. In truth, he did what was necessary to prevent the VC-NVA from invading central Vietnam and cutting the South in half. However, this forced the VC-NVA to fight the protracted war of small unit engagements. No one actually knew how to fight this style of war from the American side and took little notice of the social and political complexity of the Vietnamese.

Westmoreland was replaced by Abrams, and his job was to further Vietnamize the war and start the reduction of US military involved. Typically, when Americans and Vietnamese were paired the Vietnamese often translated or responded with what he thought the American wanted to hear, which often was not a correct understanding of the situation.

The super spy William Colby returned to Vietnam as Director of CORDS, which is the consolidation of all civilian and military personnel to be more effective all under one director. Colby used the Phoenix-CIA Program as a basis to turn defeat into victory. The plan called for the elimination of all the local VC leaders, and this was symbolized by "Cut the head off the snake and the snake dies;" in fact, this is true. However, in Vietnam, many of the leaders were stalwart members of the communities and infiltrated by the VC, which were, in fact, former members of the local community. So, in typical CIA methods, complying to laws was not necessary; without legal due process, Colby set goals of how many suspects were to be murdered- 1,800 per month along with increased "black ops" (a very insidious tactic to discredit the VC).

So here is the picture, to cut the head off of the VC the CIA brings in the military with officers in civilian clothes as Phoenix agents and awarded them with body count quotes as the master Colby Phoenix Program to defeat the VC. In fact, Phoenix was the primary means of attack program most of 1969-1972, killing 86,000 to 120,000 enemy suspects. This program was so counterproductive it was one of the primary reasons the VC-NVA ran the Americans out of Vietnam.

A lot has been written about Phoenix and a lot of it exaggerations. Phoenix did murder and torture thousands in violation of international law. The American Congress took no punitive action against the perpetrators of these crimes, possibly granting future use of these type criminal programs as it had cleared Congressional oversight. Since 9/11 the military has, by various strategies and tactics, killed thousands, if not millions, of civilians without regard for legality or concern for human life. With the failure to accomplish their mission in Iraq and Afghanistan, they still persist they know what they are doing, and I give them credit for their current status of retreating from their failures

PHOENIX-ICEX-CIA

I think you will find that all these government agencies and departments have built-in clubs or pyramidical employee relationships that are there to preserve their royalties and jobs.

Well, I was not a CIA career employee in their mists. I was one who had good contacts and a successful record of getting the job done. I was travelling 24/7 the entire country of South Vietnam dealing with a new organization just establishing all their field teams. I was working on my own support; they had no support organization. I knew the ropes, so I kept on the move looking for indications for psy-ops for Phoenix. The main CIA locations were busy writing operational plans. During this time, I had set up my psychological field operations. I did not report this because if I did they would have screwed it up with the military officers (no Vietnam experience and in civilian clothes) just coming into the country to be used as field program directors for produc-ing the 1,800 killings a month (cut the head off a snake and it dies concept). The last thing I wanted was Army officers in my field operations. I was also involved in IV corps on an ongoing development for most of five weeks. I wrote what I had developed in my 30 field operations as a psychologically directed counter-enemy field manual; I did not submit it to the CIA after see-ing the reported number of body counts coming in from the provinces' Phoe-nix operations.

Then Phoenix operatives asked me to set up a black-ops attack. It appeared that someone had found new hardware in a VC tunnel. There was only one local source for this, a Vietnamese local store owned by a family of man and wife in their 30's and two small children. The plan was to deliver some new appliances to his home, more than he could possibly afford, so it looked like a payoff. They, the CIA, had a leaflet made up in Taiwan on perfectly duplicated North Vietnamese paper ink and printing. The leaflet was a warning that this family had informed the government about the local VC; they were put to death as enemies of the people.

The whole idea was to make the VC-NVA look bad.

Some Phoenix operative shot all the family members.

I had an agent in the area who said the hardware did not come from the family's store. It was brought in from Saigon by bus; the family was not involved in any way. If this is the psy-ops they wanted me to produce and report...no way; I asked to transfer back to USAID.

All this time my field operations and Chieu Hoi-POW interrogations and interviews were producing more and better intelligence than PIC's (torture facilities), Phoenix, or military intelligence.

I liked and respected many of the senior field CIA operatives I worked with before Phoenix; I liked Evan Parker, who was in charge of the Phoenix Program. After the black-ops event...I wanted distance between me and Phoenix.

William Colby could not accept my successes so, with limited reasons to get me out of Vietnam, my reports were not acceptable. Regardless of Colby's public reputation, read the Sherman Skolnick book, *WILLIAM COLBY and CIA DIRTY TRICKS*.

Again, I repeat, Colby's directorship of the Phoenix Assassination Program, during the time it was operational, was the reason the VC strength increased and contributed to Phoenix torture and murder as much, if not more, as any reason why we were run out of Vietnam in defeat.

What I believe is the fact that America accepted the Phoenix concept as a method to deploy by our military, murder suspects, torture suspects and prisoners. I challenge any of these criminals who are involved with this type of warfare to prove it has been successful beyond its counterproductive impact on the mission involved.

The collateral death of civilians is murder, it therefore is who and how many deaths will be necessary to succeed in combat following the "Rules of Engagement." The death and wounds we rain on civilians by aircraft and artillery are inexcusable; the criminal charges go directly to our most senior officers and politicians. Unfortunately, the payback falls upon our citizens and not the ones ultimately responsible.

For the record, a lot of articles about Phoenix are exaggerated for the years 1967-1968 through the fog of war and bad reporting. I have talked with two American military officers who were assigned to Vietnam as Phoenix

Provincial Directors, both wanted, after their two-year tour 1970-1971, to talk to me 40 years later as to what Phoenix was; both claimed they sat in an office reading reports but the Phoenix was all handled by CIA staff, Vietnamese police or Vietnamese operations teams.

Military-CIA planning and reporting leave a lot to ponder.

There is more information on interrogation methods and the failure of torture in sections of this book; thousands of Vietnamese suspects were tortured to death by the CIA-Phoenix Program with no positive benefit from enemy intelligence

As to POWs taken by the military from military operations, there was torture in their first interrogation, from beatings with rifle butts or kicking and breaking ribs and arms of an enemy, who would by nature of his low rank not have any tactical information. That made no difference; beat the gook anyway. One US Captain was a legend; he liked to burn their faces with a cigarette near their eyes. All of this undisciplined conduct was tantamount to building a more determined enemy. Where was our military leadership?

As today the collateral damage of killing civilians (family members, wives, and children) continues with drone attacks. Some total our ignorance in tactics, our "Super Power" status has been defeated for going on beyond 12 years. One would think even an incompetent military would get the message; quit counting civilian children as enemy dead. However, the more I research our efforts, I doubt it.

An overview of our deployment operations would indicate the military tactics conspired with the CIA mission objectives have shown repeated failures.

A case in point. In IV CORPS, intelligence had information 15 Americans were being held prisoner in an underground bunker by the VC in a heavily fortified compound along the river. The Regional CIA Director verified there were Americans there via aerial photos. He devised a plan to raid the com-pound in a swift attack before the VC could kill them. Time was of the essence, and he requested the officers' staff of MACV Region IV to act as a blocking force while he led the RD Cadre into the compound as the attacking force. I was to provide a perimeter flank force of 75 of my Chieu Hoi APT from Region
II to avoid any suspicion of a pending action. The plan was to assemble the

next day and sweep the VC compound. It was Thursday and the attack was to be the next morning at daylight, so Agent Ward, the CIA Regional Director, went to the MACV Regional Commanding General to put the plan into effect. I had put an agent, Vietnamese, familiar with the area, into the compound and verified that there were 14 American military and one foreign contractor held prisoner in the compound.

Well, it was Thursday and the General had a tennis match scheduled, and it was steak cook-out night for the officers. The General suggested using the ARVN, and he had no time for it now. I won't repeat what Agent Ward said about the General. As far as I know, all 15 were lost.

BEGINNING OF THE END OF MY TIME IN VIETNAM

I was very successful with Chieu Hoi and military psy-ops but failed to reveal all of my contacts to the civilian (USAID) Regional Director so he could enhance his career. If he had paid more attention to cooperating with the military and CIA and working with the Vietnamese, he would have access to the top-secret assignments that I was working. It was not in my capacity to keep him informed, and apparently, the other organizations did not either.

This is one of the reasons I specify that only one command and only military be involved in the Persuasion with Relevance concept.

I think the following report on Phoenix presents sufficient data to justify my decision.

1967-1968, I was working Phoenix for Evan Parker as documents on the following pages show, and on assignments out of the CIA office in the Embassy. There are always legendary stories created during war time. I actually have the original documents substantiating my assignments. However, Parker and Colby knew I questioned the Phoenix operation of 1,800 killed per month as a quota and the torture in the PICs. Parker knew my psy-ops field operations were more effective than Phoenix, and Phoenix was actually counterproductive. The ICEX memo on 1968 Tet gave Colby the excuse to move me out of the mission. I have never met anyone who liked Colby.

The other reason I left was at the briefing for General Abrams change of command, I deviated from my rehearsed report and commented on the ineffectiveness of the six months rotation of the military. With this, the CORDS personnel were getting upset; but Abrams came up to the lectern, shook my hand and said he agreed, "Good, honest report," and he was there to close out the American involvement. He also asked if I could find the rocket launching sites that were pounding Saigon. I said I probably could, but those civilian bureaucrats who overheard that would never let that happen. I had the connections and access to get that information; it would have saved lives, American and Vietnamese. I would assume the CIA-Military torture procedures were not producing results because I knew they had taken many "suspects" from what they thought were the locations. Counter-battery radar can determine direction but not range, and the VC fired a homemade mortar round at the same time as a rocket. The counter-battery picked up the range from it. They killed 42 elementary school students and two teachers with one 155 artillery round. Stupid is as stupid does.

I had a lovely wife and four small children; it was time to let go.

[133]

THIS IS THE REPORT THAT ENDED MY POTEN-TIAL CAREER WITH THE DEPARTMENT OF STATE

PERFORMANCE EVALUATION REPORT   USAID VIETNAM Page _____

Harry D. Wagner	William Law	November 30, 1967 to August 9, 1968
Rated Officer	Rating Officer	Period Covered

PART III

    Mr. Wagner presents an excellent appearance, is well informed, has an effective and pleasant manner, and makes a fine initial impression. During the rated period he was instructed to conduct an extensive experiment to determine if a permanent PsyOps specialist on the PHOENIX Staff could make constructive contribution concerning aspects of counter-insurgency operations. In the course of this effort he travelled widely in several Corps areas, participated in psyops in each, contributing to local planning and indoctrination, and assisted in local liaison with GVN PsyOps officers. There seems no doubt that Mr. Wagner knows the psyops technique and that he cooperated with existing PsyOps agencies in areas visited. However, the overall result of his activities, and the impact of his reporting, which was fragmentary, did not support the need for a permanent PsyOps specialist on the PHOENIX Staff.

After 17 months of fieldwork with the Chieu Hoi system, Psy-ops, and with access to CIA, MACV, and SITREPS country-wide, plus the Embassy assignments such as the counting of and estimating enemy dead from Tet country wide working with all the Army photographers...I think my estimates of the situation were correct.

But I violated the first Tenet of Government Bureaucracy: Don't admit mistakes or failures!

When you have days counting the bodies of hundreds of dead old men, women, and children who have been caught in crossfires, it would seem to be the truth should prevail. But often careers are based on distortions and lies. Why is this allowed and continued to this day?

Do we know the casualties count for Iraq or Afghanistan?

The following evaluation was written by Evan J. Parker, Jr. He was the senior CIA officer William Colby chose as the director of Phoenix. Parker was considered to be the expert in "unconventional warfare." I had little contact with him; I believe he knew what I was doing, and it was counter to the Colby Phoenix Murder and Torture Program. According to Parker himself, he was uncomfortable saluting and following orders in the Phoenix Program, which he considered "tragically ineffective, if not hideous." His rating of my performance at Phoenix was not anything close to his self-evaluation as head of Phoenix. At least I was out in the field, where the war was, actively looking for the most effective use of Phoenix, via Chieu Hoi defectors rather than murder and torture.

PERFORMANCE EVALUATION REPORT   USAID VIETNAM Page _____

Harry D. Wagner	Evan J. Parker, Jr.	November 30, 1967 to August 9, 1968
Rated Officer	Reviewing Officer	Period Covered

PART IV

    Mr. Wagner's primary duty was to develop doctrine, draw up procedures, design operations, devise evaluation techniques and generally stimulate optimum use of psychological action in the exploitation phase of the PHOENIX program, in accordance with a letter of instruction.

    Mr. Wagner served with the program approximately six months, both in Saigon in a staff capacity and in II, III and IV Corps on temporary duty as a psyops staff advisor and consultant. During this period the PHOENIX program was in transition from the organizational to the operational phase, but a number of participating elements already were engaged quite actively in exploitation operations. Mr. Wagner gave freely of his time, advice and guidance; offered useful ideas and constructive suggestions, and contributed to the preparation of policy guidances and field operational plans. But while Mr. Wagner stimulated interest in psyops through his extensive personal meetings with US and Vietnamse field personnel, he did not produce the SOPs and other written materials which had been envisioned and expected of him.

    Mr. Wagner is intelligent, highly motivated, and seriously interested -- as a practical idealist -- in doing something for the people of the less developed areas. He enjoyed being among the local people, particularly in the rural areas and "in the street" in the cities and towns. He was quick to critize on-going programs, but his observations were thoughtful and honest. He was able to recognize and size up opportunities for psyops action, and to suggest plans and techniques; however, he did not seem ever to be able to carry these ideas through to a completed action or completed project.

    I have come to believe that the field of psyops is intriguing and interesting to Mr. Wagner, but that their detailed and practical application are not his forte.

This is my staff who produced the fragmentary reporting. The lady did not speak English. One day she did not show for work at my Nha Trang Chieu Hoi office. I actually had to get an armed force to safely escort her to work and with two American friends chase six VC out of her family home. She lived less than a half mile away; that might have contributed to fragmentary reporting. Oh yes, we only had electricity 1.5 to 2 hours a day. I worked in the field, not Saigon. The action was in the field up until Tet '68; then the enemy brought it into town.

Even now as then, you had to shake your head and smile at the wonderment of government.

The following pages are examples of operational reports and memos for the Phoenix-ICEX Program.

C-O-N-F-I-D-E-N-T-I-A-L

ICEX OPERATIONAL AID NO. 3

SUBJECT: Cordon and Search Operations   11 October 1967

REFERENCES: A. MACV DIR 381-41, dated 9 July 1967

B. ICEX Memorandum No. 1 dated 11 August 1967

1. (C) **PURPOSE**: This operational aid is intended to provide additional guidance to improve the effectiveness of cordon and search operations in the attack on the Viet Cong (VC) infrastructure.

2. (C) **DISCUSSION**:

a. A desired objective in a cordon and search operation is the eventual pacification of the hamlet, village, or area. Pacification depends upon the identification and elimination of the Viet Cong infrastructure, main force and guerrilla units. Experience has proven that it serves little purpose to drive organized Viet Cong military units out of an area without eliminating the VC infrastructure. As military units sweep an area, entrapped Viet Cong either bury their weapons and mingle with the population, conceal themselves in tunnels, or move into nearby jungles or mountains only to infiltrate back into the area upon the departure of friendly military units. Unless all these elements are eliminated, the Viet Cong is allowed to maintain its military and political control over the population, thus preventing the population from being firmly committed to the Government of Vietnam (GVN).

b. A study of several recent cordon and search operations revealed that large amounts of material and manpower are being expended and relatively few VC are being detected, captured, or killed as a result of these operations. The lack of good intelligence, failure to exploit available sources of information on the hamlet, village or district, failure to properly utilize GVN personnel, employment of poor questioning techniques, and improper security practices were the more significant reasons for the limited results achieved on these operations.

c. Effective cordon and search operations, utilizing all locally available intelligence, have the effect of depriving the Viet Cong of "sanctuary among the population",

C-O-N-F-I-D-E-N-T-I-A-L

GROUP-4
DOWNGRADED AT 3 YEAR
INTERVALS; DECLASSIFIED
AFTER 12 YEARS

[138]

C-O-N-F-I-D-E-N-T-I-A-L

one of the mainstays of guerrilla war. Such operations, utilizing carefully prepared blacklists and search techniques, may also be expected to have considerable psychological impact on the population, in that the Allied operational units are specifically searching for specifically identified people.

3. (C) <u>CONCEPT OF OPERATIONS</u>:

 a. General: The following specific measures appropriate for cordon and search operations are aimed at the VC infrastructure. They are identified in terms of planning, execution and follow-up or after action requirements. It is recognized that these are not all inclusive, that not all will apply to every unit or area of operation, and that some units are employing most or all of these practices and accomplishing desired objectives.

 b. Planning:

  (1) During preliminary planning, consideration must be given to exploiting every available source of information on the target. In addition to tasking the Combined Intelligence Center Vietnam (CICV) and other US and GVN military agencies for information on the target, the following individuals or agencies should be contacted:

   (a) Province advisor for Police Special Branch (PSB) for blacklists and collated studies on the VC from PSB, from the Provincial Interrogation Center and for PSB assistance in the operation. PSB should be tasked to prepare their support, drawing in addition from the Census Grievance Study Center, for census overlays, hamlet books, and so on. The Provincial Intelligence Coordination Committee (PICC) should be utilized to accomplish Vietnamese agency coordination. Information, blacklists, census overlays and studies should be requested on several different hamlets or villages in order to select the most promising target and not disclose the primary area of interest. Determination of the most promising target may depend on the mission of the unit planning the operation; however, target selection should normally be based on an analysis of collated information which indicates that the Viet Cong are in the area, and they can be identified through the use of a blacklist, "mugg books", VC census overlays, identifiers, guides, or a combination of them. Requests for studies should be submitted not only for

C-O-N-F-I-D-E-N-T-I-A-L

specific operations, but should be requested, maintained, and annotated on a continuing basis to assist in the selection of targets for future operations.

(b) The Province S2 advisor for military order of battle information contained and collated in the Sector Operations Intelligence Center (SOIC).

(c) The ICEX Coordinator in the District Operations and Intelligence Coordinating Center (DOICC), in districts where a DOICC has been established, for VC infrastructure and other information on the VC.

(d) The District S2 and the District Police Chief, in areas where a DOICC has not been established, through coordination with the Senior Sub Sector advisor for information on VC personalities and order of battle information.

(e) The Provincial Chieu Hoi Center to select and furnish Hoi Chanhs formerly from the target area to assist in the operation by identifying VC members and suspects. Police Special Branch should be tasked not only to obtain suitable Hoi Chanhs from the Center, but also to review their arrested and convicted prisoners, for knowledgeable and cooperative individuals. Hoi Chanhs may also be obtained from Census Grievance and from Province S2. Consideration should also be given to select Hoi Chanhs from areas other than the target area to draw attention away from the primary target and reduce the possibility of compromise. Hoi Chanhs who will not be used may be returned to the center shortly after the operation has begun. In using Hoi Chanhs or other identifiers from the local population, arrangements should be made to place them in a covered vehicle or other suitable location with a policeman where they can observe members of the hamlet or village without being seen. One method is to have inhabitants file by a certain point for an identification card check where they can be observed by the Hoi Chanh or identifier.

(2) Military operations such as cordon and search, offer access to areas hitherto denied to GVN police and US military intelligence personnel, thus providing an **Opportunity** to recruit informants and organize informant

C-O-N-F-I-D-E-N-T-I-A-L

nets in these newly opened areas. It is therefore important and desirable that arrangements be made to have GVN Police Special Branch personnel participate in these operations and prepare to institute widespread and effective informant operations to provide expanded coverage of these areas to identify VC personalities and monitor their activities for possible exploitation, neutralization or elimination. Selection of the National Police Special Branch for the task of instituting widespread informant nets does not preclude military intelligence agencies from recruiting informants to meet requirements of their mission, but provides a greater degree of permanency to the program because of the Police Special Branch mission and the long range pacification objectives.

(3) Aerial and ground reconnaissance of the target area should be coordinated to preclude repeated reconnaissance of the area by brigade, battalion, and company personnel and possibly disclosing friendly interest in the area.

(4) The wide use of aliases by the Viet Cong, the use of incomplete blacklists, and the problems involved in attempting to identify a Viet Cong political leader or guerrilla from a blacklist without diacritical markings or, a blacklist containing only a name and date and place of birth, has often reduced the effectiveness of an otherwise well planned operation. Information from all available sources must be collected, collated, placed in useable format for use by both US and GVN participating elements, and readily accessible during the operation. In addition to using a collated blacklist and census overlays, dossiers on the approximately twenty key VC functionaries in the district should be assembled, the information extracted from the dossiers and held accessible during the operation to assist in screening and interviewing inhabitants who may have knowledge of them. Efforts should also be directed to obtain photographs of these selected functionaries, and to obtain information on their relatives for inclusion in their dossiers for use during and after the operation.

    c. Execution:

        (1) Establish a Command Post on the ground where the operation can be centrally coordinated and

C-O-N-F-I-D-E-N-T-I-A-L

C-O-N-F-I-D-E-N-T-I-A-L

controlled, to serve as a central collection point for all captured documents and photographs, and as a central reaction point for information developed during the operation. There have been instances where personnel have kept captured documents and photographs in their possession for turn in at a later date in expectation of an award and for other reasons.

(2) National Police personnel should complete, if census data does not exist in police files, a basic registration card (Annex A) on all persons over 15 years of age, and also photograph these individuals. If time is not available to complete this action, then it should be limited to persons who may be of possible future interest to the National Police e.g., relatives, friends, and VC sympathizers. Photographs will be printed in two copies; one copy pasted to the registration card and the other placed in the hamlet book for possible use in subsequent operations, and for identification by Hoi Chanhs and informants.

(3) Prepare blacklist cards (Annex B) on all newly developed persons who should be placed on the blacklist.

(4) Ensure that screeners question relatives, friends, neighbors, and other knowledgeable individuals of VC functionaries who are operating in the area concerning their whereabouts, activities, movements and expected return.

(5) Establish interview rooms or areas where selected individuals may be interviewed privately, but not necessarily together by Police Special Branch personnel and military intelligence personnel. Efforts should be made to convince these persons that they can cooperate without being detected by the other inhabitants. The availability of monetary awards for certain types of information and equipment should also be discussed during the interview.

(6) Supervise the search teams and ensure that every house is searched systematically and completely and every possible concealment device is checked.

(7) Ensure that blacklists and Census Grievance overlays are annotated with information obtained

C-O-N-F-I-D-E-N-T-I-A-L

C-O-N-F-I-D-E-N-T-I-A-L

during the operation, and that the information is provided to the originating agencies to update their files.

    (8) Forward all information concerning the VC infrastructure to the District or Province ICEX Coordinator for inclusion in district or province files. Information concerning VC committee meetings will be forwarded to the nearest District or Province ICEX Coordinator as soon as possible for exploitation, if it is not possible for participating elements to react to the information.

4. (C) <u>CONCLUSIONS</u>: The goal of a search operation should be to <u>return from</u> the operation with a reasonable dividend or profit to compensate for resources invested. A means to collect this dividend or profit is to develop a good intelligence base on the target prior to the operation. The importance of the elimination of the Viet Cong infrastructure in conjunction with military operations cannot be overemphasized.

2 Annexes
as

EVAN J. PARKER, JR.
Director, ICEX Staff

C-O-N-F-I-D-E-N-T-I-A-L

18 January 1968

MEMORANDUM FOR: Director, ICEX Staff

SUBJECT: Thirty Day Review

Background:

    The last 30 working days I have spent in Saigon, except for one field trip to three provinces in IV Corps, working in the ICEX office. Most of this time has been spent reading ICEX material and familiarizing myself with the program or making liaison with other agencies. It has been impossible during this time to collate the right type of information which I consider necessary to plan polwar (psyops) activities to fit the ICEX structure. The Saigon office is organized to supervise and administer the total ICEX program. It is not an intelligence collect center suitable for focusing on the polwar activities. When many of the initial growth and administration problems are complete this situation could change. I think that once we have additional field experience and have tested some of our ideas, such as those suggested by Jim Ward, a centralized function could be developed that would benefit the program.

Situation:

    Intelligence at the targetted level is the base for all polwar ICEX activities, this is only available in detail at the province level and below within ICEX. There is a report from Binh Thuan which is ideally suited for polwar exploitation. With this type of report from the field and some on-site study, much could be accomplished (attachment). I think Jim Ward's paper gave some excellent ideas but until they can be applied to field situations such as those in Binh Thuan we haven't proved our concept. We are saddled with ideas but lack the proof which is necessary to produce doctrine.

    The essential factors to prove our polwar ideas are in the field, probably within the PRU activities. Rather than request additional report requirements to ICEX on reporting polwar (psyops) situations, I plan to survey several provinces especially the DIOCC and PRU teams to find the most likely combinations with which to work.

It is possible to apply propaganda to any situation, as is currently being done by the careful planning for PRU operations. These operations can generate good polwar (psyops) just by the finesse in the way they are carried out. If we can insert our ideas on polwar into these PRU activities in such a manner so the results are gauged, I think we can come up with some much needed experience. These experiences written up as guidelines for ICEX polwar

Proposal:

I would like to offer the following as to my next 30 days activities.

    1) Visit Binh Thuan next week to follow up attached report.

    2) Attend the II Corps ICEX Coordinators meeting in Nha Trang on 21 January.

    3) Visit Quang Duc to follow-up the IV Corps request on the KKK situation in Can Duc.

    4) Spend three weeks traveling in IV Corps to concentrate on their polwar potential.

    5) Locate some adequate housing in Saigon so I can exploit several ICEX/polwar counterpart associations

                                  Harry D. Wagner
                                  ICEX/Psyops

cc: PAD

Despite this enthusiastic report, Phoenix proved to be a failure. Phoenix was one of the last efforts to salvage victory for the Americans in Vietnam.

Operation Phoenix

President Thieu has strongly endorsed an intelligence operation designed to find and neutralize the estimated 60,000 to 100,000 members of the Viet Cong shadow government. This is the latest in a series of such attempts. All the others either were subverted by the Viet Cong or floundered because of disinterest or jurisdictional disputes among the several intelligence services of the Vietnamese government.

Thus, the somewhat belated Thieu endorsement of Operation Phoenix is a welcome development. It means, one must hope, that the government leadership has at long last recognized the importance of uprooting this alternative government to their own, which controls guerrilla bands, collects taxes, orders assassinations, sets up front organizations, recruits soldiers, disseminates propaganda, and otherwise exercises firm control over large areas of South Vietnam.

Unless this shadow government is eliminated beforehand, any political settlement of the Vietnam conflict will not be worth the paper it is written on. The one man-one vote formula, for instance, would allow all Viet Cong who forswore violence and accepted the constitution to vote and hold office. Under these ground rules, however, the shadow government could engage in subversion on a large scale and, of course, be well positioned to attempt a coup d'etat.

Operation Phoenix appears to be an effective response to the problem. In theory, the operatives of the three Vietnamese intelligence services, the Police Special Branch, the Defense Department, and the Army, are working in tandem out of District Intelligence and Operations Centers in about 200 key districts. Supposedly inter-service rivalries are being laid aside, political intrigues abandoned, and intelligence information shared. United States intelligence reportedly has been playing a prominent advisory role.

It is claimed that 6,000 members of the shadow government have been captured or killed, but this leaves thousands of Viet Cong officials burrowed in. Operation Phoenix, like all intelligence operations, is a dirty business, but it is a necessary one, never more than now. It should not be permitted to fail.

CHAPTER 6

CHIEU HOI

The Chieu Hoi program was unique to the Vietnam War; it was supported by the military for reasons I will explain. The devastation of the war was the action that made defection a better choice than dying. The amazing thing is that it was a program involved in all aspects of field operations by the military and all the civilian pacification programs. It was a major source of intelligence on the enemy as to leadership and operational locations of the Viet Cong. I worked with over 3,500 Viet Cong and 25 NVA in just one province and recently have found out that at least two of the NVA were actually Chinese Army officers working as advisors to the NVA and VC.

When I arrived in Vietnam 1966 September the program had been put on a high priority and was in the throes of expanding without much field support. My first duty assignment was made by an Army Colonel at the American Embassy; I had not officially reported to USAID. I became the Regional Chieu Hoi Advisor, a lucky break for me because the program was fully involved with all the different military and CIA.

The Chieu Hoi Center, located in Binh Dinh Province, had been inoperable for three years. No one had been able to get it started because of contract disputes and dishonesty. By the time I arrived, there were 3,500 Hoi Chan (defectors) sitting on a soccer field for a week without any facilities, as the result of a large military sweep of Phu Cat. There were several Filipinos hold-ing on trying to organize some facilities, so we got to work. We used the Hoi Chan as labor and I was frequently working amongst them. They were more human than I imagined. I shared meals with them and slept in the same quarters while we were working. I was able to get it up and running efficiently in six months. It required a lot of field time, whereas the USAID assignments were stuck under the oversight of the bureaucratic career enhancement political USAID directors who wanted all reports to promote their valuable administrative management. Chieu Hoi was a Vietnamese government program so I had a lot of leeway with what I reported.

After 44 years it is now interesting to read some articles written about the work I did in Vietnam but I didn't know I was doing it. The rewriting of the Vietnam War is unbelievable as the book *Phoenix* by Douglas Valentine portrays. Valentine was not in Vietnam, nor was he involved in Phoenix.

Check my credentials (chapter 9); how could I have missed the activities that Valentine claimed happened from 1966-1968? With my senior rank, security clearances, and writing the White House weekly report on Chieu Hoi, in control of all military and civilian psy-ops for a third of Vietnam, and even my CORDS rank as a General officer in military intelligence. Is it possible I could have missed so much for 22 months?

With the change of command from Westmoreland to Abrams and the closing down of the war for American involvement anything could have happened. But some of Frank Scotton's Vietnamese personnel in 1975 were sponsored here in the USA from Guam by my family; we shared our home for six months with one of his top operators and family. I heard his side of the war as a former VC and Chieu Hoi.

William Colby and CIA are primarily responsible for the death of thousands of South Vietnamese civilians guilty of no crime other than being Vietnamese.

Chieu Hoi --- A Winning Program

Command
Information
Pamphlet
Number 13-66
October 1966

****

MACV Office
of
Information
APO 96222

RELAXATION WHILE LEARNING AND WORKING

The long hours and stress would get to you; my way of relaxing and catch-ing up on sleep was, I think, unique. I, my interpreter, and two or three APT would find a hamlet of 15 or 20 different families on a small off the beaten path, un-militarized and of no particular importance. We would ask permis-sion to stay and most greeted us as friends (no uniforms). My interpreter and I had day watch, the APT had night watch with 12-hour shifts. We had total relaxation, got some sound sleep and watched the people go about their work, like a commune. I liked to play with the kids and often was awarded the task of babysitting. We brought to the hamlet salt, fish sauce, cooking utensils, knives, and several sturdy buckets along with two tennis balls. We played catch with the kids and sometimes stickball. The children had never seen a ball and didn't know how to throw or catch. Sometimes we would have games between the children and mothers. The mothers especially enjoyed this. The games brought some joy to people who struggled daily for survival, and some much-needed recreation for myself. My interpreter would tell them who I was and the APT would talk about Chieu Hoi; that's all—no questions.

Little girl drawing water at communal well.

We learned what they would accept and what they thought. It was mostly the same in the rural un-militarized areas. In the militarized hamlets it was a different story; there was the feeling of tension and distrust. It was very diffi-cult to connect with them. We would try to define their problems and offer advice and arrange for medical team visits and cover other shortages. In the greater sense, these were more obligated as military outposts than the typical Vietnamese hamlet or village.

[150]

We had started an APT work self-help concept program to give assistance to the villages to reduce tension and distrust. I thought it had great potential, but I was transferred to Saigon and the Embassy before I could get it functional.

As primitive as conditions were, compared to urban American living, these hamlets were a paradise. To watch these families, working together, sharing and caring for each other, getting the required work done; it just played out as if orchestrated.

A typical hamlet in rural Vietnam.

It made you think what right we had by force of violence to make decisions for many of these hamlets that they didn't need, understand, or want. They could have advanced into a better, more technological life in their own time. We are the largest exponent of violence in the world today. Why?

This picture is from my files with the following notation taped to the back:

CHIEU HOI   DARLAC PROVINCE

Sing Along with Ong vo

This is a picture of a group of Hoi Chanh at the Darlac Province Chieu Hoi Center. The Hoi Chanh are shown making a tape recording of Tet songs and messages. The gentleman at the extreme right is Mr. Do Quang Nguyen, chief of programming at Radio BanMeThuot, who is very enthusiastic in this project. The tape is presently played by him over his program VOICE OF BANMETHUOT. The tape is addressed to their former comrades who are still in the "countryside" and invites them to take advantage of the Tet holiday to rally to the national cause.

The man playing the mandolin is Hoi Chanh Vo Hou. He is being eyed by the Chieu Hoi Service Office for a job of arranging musical and other cultural presentations after his release from the center.

o.c.e.

2 Feb., '67

When it comes to psychologically directed programs, the Chieu Hoi was the largest and most effective in Vietnam.

If properly managed it was a terrific source for intelligence.

I am standing with Major Tan, the highest-ranking North Vietnamese officer who defected to Chieu Hoi. He was in South Vietnam for four years. He was the Deputy Province Administrator of Lang Son, a province strategically located in North Vietnam that borders with China.

And from this book, you will see it touched on everything about life in Vietnam and that made it a very interesting assignment. I was the Senior Advisor for Region II and IFFV Military; it was like running a large hospitality business. A Vietnamese program fully staffed and budgeted with support from the American USAID/CORDS. USAID was to be the motivation and not the control, with an added function to convince the US military to take defec-tors instead of killing them. It functioned as a psy-ops program fully equipped to produce and deliver leaflets and sound; the range of activity was country-wide to include all military units, American and Vietnamese. So, we spent part of our time working with the VN side and the rest with the military promoting Chieu Hoi in the field with the US units. The position of Regional Chief was to keep it running corruption free and conducting operations with integrity.

Chieu Hoi was the most active psychological operational program in Vietnam.

Region II processed 12,000 to 18,000 Chieu Hoi enemy defectors a year. We operated 12 compounds containing up to 3,500 former enemy. During my tour, I worked with 9,000 VC/NVA defectors. We operated interrogation screening and exploitation programs. By utilizing the Chieu Hoi interrogation reports, I provided military intelligence reports not only to the US military, but also promoting Chieu Hoi and Psychological Operations along with tactical intelligence on the enemy to the Korean Army, Philippine Army, and Thailand Army units positioned in Vietnam. We strictly followed the Vietnamese instructions and avoided any torture or abuse.

I also worked country wide all four regions on special assignment from the Embassy on unit defections, especially for North Vietnamese units. My job was to encourage American, Korean, and Vietnamese to taking defectors as Chieu Hoi and avail their units of the trained manpower as scouts, APT, and guides for combat units. My job was not a desk job; it was to cover one-third of the country of Vietnam in Region II and at times the whole country of South Vietnam. This was not the job description I was employed to perform, but a lot more interesting.

By the time *the bureaucrat* got settled in with his predetermined Washington-devised solutions to the Vietnam war, I had been working with IFFV Command, Special Forces Headquarters, VN Police Special Branch at a national level, most of the region's VN and MACV Provincial Chiefs, and the Region II CIA personnel, all a mutual aid society. I spent as much time as I could get away with in the field. T*he bureaucrat* wanted staff where he could see them, which would have been unproductive in my scope of work (but my programs were high priority ones reporting to the White House in a separate report). I had established very productive interlocking relationships with the above-mentioned groups; we had become mutually supportive and trusting (very unusual for such a mission).

When Chieu Hoi became a "White House priority program" every bureau-crat in the mission wanted in on it, but when it meant dealing with the Vietnamese management or doing the dirty field work required in the unsecured areas, they were nowhere in sight. There were two of us in the Regional office. Leon Kahn was one of the best, if not the best, coworker ever and a great friend.

There is a point to be made here. You cannot mix civilian agencies in military deployed missions.

The practice of assigning career bureaucrats to positions of authority into military operations to build their careers should stop. The military should develop a separate position for the bureaucrats so their involvement does not impair military operations. The field manual I assembled based on my field operations was written in the Phoenix Saigon office. I made the choice not to submit it to the CIA because Phoenix was developing into nothing more than "Murder Incorporated" and counting killings and body counting to enhance military careers. I have been asked why I didn't have a copy. You risk your life taking papers out of a CIA Field Office; I put it in the burn bag.

LIFE WITH THE CHIEU HOI APT

Armed Propaganda Team

I was recruited to be an advisor to a Province Chief in matters concerning American support as to join programs in his province. Not in my wildest dreams would you find me in black pajamas with an AK somewhere in the jungle with 15 former enemy VC, all armed to provide security for me.

Actually, we were setting up an operation on a small hamlet to see what the impact of our psy-ops program had on the population. We selected hamlets and villages that had not been exposed to American military. Of the 15 Team members, 10 were to be the Shield and 5 the Spear Team, plus me. The impact was always the same whether the population was 60 or 600; reactions were noticeably the same when there was no aggression or hostilities We tried our approach with me in black, in US military uniform, and in casual civilian clothing. Always the civilian clothing was accepted better.

These small hamlets and villages were clear during the day, but at night were frequently visited by VC and occasionally by NVA with VC. Our program required a stay of five days and nights. Out of 30 field test operations, only twice did the villagers feel it necessary to move me and the five Spear Team to safety out of the village of 250 inhabitants. This was caused by the approach of a military VC arrow patrol approaching with a senior VC officer. (The VC arrow patrol tactic as a formation never ceased to defy American countermeasures to it). So, in total darkness, we were led away to safety. The Vietnamese I worked with were outstanding. They wanted the war to end, and they never could fathom how it became so big and so violent. Any change in government would have little effect on the population, being mostly rural and partially isolated.

Our conversations were about family and lifestyle, not religion or government. They appreciated every opportunity to learn, and this caused us to look at what we could add to the Spear Team for the villagers. We found a simple manual powered lift pump made out of bamboo, a simple way to split bamboo, and snatch blocks (pulleys), multi sheaves to make lifting easier.

We made mistakes and we learned from them. On occasion, our field operations caused loss of life of villagers as punishment for our visit; we developed ways to prevent this. At night we started staying with the family with the most family members in the VC.

The APT, they liked making friends with the Americans on an equal basis of trust and respect.

APT (Armed Propaganda Team) in traditional black clothing.

They don't look like much but were my security while out in the field operations; they were a big store of knowledge for procedures in Psychologi-cal Operations. They are wearing black clothing, which was traditional garb of the Vietnamese. The APT (Chieu Hoi) was concerned for my safety wearing my American clothing when I was in the field with them on Psychological Operations in contested enemy areas. I explained it was to separate me as being a guest in their country, and they were the true members of the country. I was there because I wanted to help the Vietnamese and to stop the violence. Treat them like a friend, and you have a brother.

```
REPUBLIC OF VIETNAM
         -O-
MINISTRY OF INFORMATION
AND CHIEU HOI
         -O-
KHANH HOA CHIEU HOI OFFICE
```

Nhatrang, March 24, 1967

No # 967/CH/KH

TO : Mr. Harry D Wagner
     Region II Chieu-Hoi Chief,
     Nhatrang.

FROM : Nguyen Quang Tho
       Chieu-Hoi Chief, Khanh-Hoa

    This is respectfully offered to you for you in your field trip.

    It was made by tailoring trainee returnees in the Khanh-Hoa Chieu-Hoi Center - clothing was provided by CARE, Nhatrang in the ceremony held for distribution of two sewing-machines at the Center.

Signed ; <u>NGUYEN QUANG THO</u>

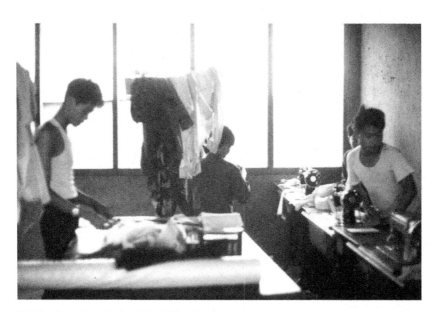

Hoi Chanh working in the Chieu Hoi tailor shop.

After we failed in Vietnam over 2,000 of them were executed by the VC. I am telling this now because the military did not make it public.

With these men, our loyalty to each other was solid. They would have stood between me and a bullet, as we Americans were jumping off roofs to helicopters to escape.

Lesson learned: Population preferred visitors who were not military in appearance, with causal conduct, open and friendly to all, and acknowledged the village and population as good and gracious to strangers.

CHIEU HOI SUCCESS

The following documents highlight the success that came with the Chieu Hoi Program. The telegram was received at Region II's Chieu Hoi Center. It refers to a very successful operation completed by a Chieu Hoi defector against the VC. It is a very typical scenario of the success we found working with the Vietnamese.

TELEGRAM

FLASH

    TO: - UNDER SECRETARY FOR CHIEU HOI, SAIGON REGION II CH REP-RESENTATIVE, PLEIKU

    FM: KHANH HOA CHIEU HOI CHIEF.

    NO # 1085/TCH/KH/CD OF APRIL 6 1967.

    YOU ARE INFORMED THAT ON THE 2ND OF APRIL, 1967, RETURNEE NGO-THYEN, A VC DISTRICT LIASION CELL LEADER IN VAN-NINH, TURNED HIMSELF IN TO THE GVN WITH ONE CARBINE OWING TO THE BEST INTERROGATION AND EXPLOITATION OF VAN NINH DISTRICT CHIEU HOI CHIEF, KHANH HOA PROVINCE? ON APRIL 5, 1967 HE GUIDED A LOCAL FORCE UNIT TO LAY OUT AN OPERATION TO HOC CH/M VC SECRET BASE CQ0411083 IN AN AREA OF VAN NINH DISTRICT AND HE LOCATED A VC CADRE OF WEAPONS AND FOOD. HIS ACTION RESULTED IN CAPTURING 34 MAUSERS, 5 ANTI-TANKS, 5,000 ROUNDS OF AMMO AND 200Kg OF RICE. MAJOR PROVINCE

CHIEF OF KHANH HOA WENT TO VAN NINH ON APRIL 6, 1967 TO AWARD THE LOCAL TROOP AND PRESENTED A GALLANTRY CROSS TO MRLE VAN-MAU? ACTING CHIEU HOI CHIEF AT VAN NINH DISTRICT AND AN AMOUNT OF $VN 2,000.00 TO RETURNEE NGO-THU-YEN THIS OFFICE IS MAKING A REQUEST FOR A NATIONAL LEVEL AWARD FOR HIS SPECIAL SERVICE MISSION.

S/ NGUYEN QUANG THO

CC:
- MR. HARRY DWAGNER.
- MAJOR MHURWITZ
- OCO, PROVREP., NHATRANG
    "FOR INFORMATION"

CORDS, BAO LOC
25 July 1967

On 20 July 1967, at 12:30 in the afternoon, a stocky young man clad in black pajamas flagged down a three-man bearing ARVN jeep at Dai Nga Hamlet along route 20 some six kilometers east of Bao Loc town, capitol of Lam-Dong Province. The head man in the jeep asked 25 year-old Nguyen Dao where he was going and the reply was that he is a VC and wants to surrender.

At ten o'clock that same day his trek to freedom started some five kilometers away when he, unnoticed, fled from his unit, the C-740 Company formerly C-210 Company operating in that province. He ran and ran as fast as he could to the direction of the highway. He brought with him an M-1 Rifle and 88 rounds partly due to the claim in the three GVN leaflets he tucked inside his secret pocket on rewards for surrendered weapons and partly to fight it out once cornered by his ersthwhile comrades.

Hoi-Chanh Dao was brought to the ARVN headquarters for immediate interrogation. Moved by the fair treatment accorded him by the ARVN soldiers he volunteered the information that on the next day at 2:00 PM his unit was to make liaison and coordinate with elements of the 186 VC Battalion at the Tu Quy Plantation and there rehearse the attack previously planned on an ARVN unit. Earlier in the morning of his surrender his company was already well-briefed on such plans by the company commander using a sand table for effect. It depicted a tea plantation and a nearby stream with a muddy area. Another future target of these combined forces was to be the Revolutionary Development Area 8 and 9 of Tan Phat village located at about 5 kilometers northeast of Bao-Loc.

The 1st Battalion 44th Regiment ARVN Bao-Loc and Ranger Units moved fast on this tip and true enough the rendezvous took place. With are support of four choppers and four gunships from the US Airforce stationed at both Bao-Loc and Ban Me Thuot the surprised enemy forces were routed accounting for the following:

    38 VCs Dead
    1 Carbine
    1 Generator for AN/GRC9 Radio
    3 Telephone Sets TA/43
  4000 Meters of Telephone Wires
      1 Aiming Sight of 82 MM Mortar of Red Chinese make
      4 Trench shovels
    28 Magazines BAR
     7 Pieces of TNT

    1 M-26 Grenade
  23 Stick Grenade
    6 Rounds Mortar 82 MM
    9 Rounds 60 Mortar
    3 Boxes of Detonator
 200 Assorted Cartridges
  10 Rounds M-79 Grenade Launcher
    3 Bags of Rice
       Clothese and Documents and Pictures

Nguyen Dao was Asst Sqd Leader of the 7th, 3rd Platoon, C-740 Company. He hails from Quang-Ngai Province. He served the VCs for the past three years.

Meanwhile, Dao has received VN$3,000 form the Province Chief for the weapons surrendered, USAID items such as blankets, mosquito nets, two pairs of clothing, cooking oil and a sewing and stationery kit from the Chieu-Hoi Chief plus VN$1,100 for initial allowance. He will be richer by a few thousand more piastres as soon as his contribution to the Tu Quy operations, considered one of the most successful thereabouts, can be determined.

Incidentally, Nguyen Dao appears in the Chieu-Hoi Office list of active VCs operating in the province.

OUTLINE OF BRIEFING MR WAGNER, OCO GAVE TO GENERAL ABRAMS ON 8 MAY 1967

I Several points of interest in the Region II Chieu Hoi Program:

    A. Philosophy of the "Open Arms" Program dictates that it is a GVN civilian program.

    B. The Chieu Hoi Program requires the full support of all US/civilian, US/military, Free World Forces, and ARVN.

        1. ARVN does not actively support the Program in Region II.

        2. There is some evidence of a lack of knowledge of the Chieu Hoi Program in US Military units. With the continual relation of US forces, it is difficult to keep them aware of the advantages to them of the Chieu Hoi Program.

C. Returnees: During 1966, Region II had 9,068 Hoi Chieu Hoi which was 46% of the National total. Since 1 January 1967, there have been 4,434 returnees reported in Region II, an increase of approximately 30% over the same period last year.

    1. A current estimate for 1967 would be 12,000 returnees for CY 1967 in Region

    2. Our goal for CY was 20,000 returnees; this was based upon the large number which rallied in Binh Dinh during 1966 as a result of Operation Irving.

D. Prospect for 1967: The Chieu Hoi Program has developed enough statistics to reflect that the number of returnees is directly related to the tactical operations conducted by US Military units. The sustained military operations will produce more returnees than the Search and Destroy operations, particularly those in dense population areas. The basis for this is the ROK/US Operations in Phu Yen and the US Battalion in Binh Thuan.

E. Region II probably has more Hoi Chanh being utilized by military units than any other Corps area, but it has been impossible to get reports back from units as to numbers and successes of this exploitation.

II Exploitation:

A. Less than 10% of the Hoi Chanh returned to US/ROK or ARVN combat forces, 90% of the returnees are received through the ARVN civil channels. During the first three months of this year only 47% of the returnees in Region II were interrogated, 11% used for psy-ops and 3% exploited in combat or police operations. This is unsatisfactory and we are working to rectify this situation.

III Armed Propaganda Teams:

A. The official GVN Guidelines have been released by the MICH. It is our opinion that the APT is one of the most valuable products generated in this war. Its potential has hardly been tapped. This program should receive maximum emphasis.

IV The four primary Chieu Hoi Activities

    A. Inducement (psy-ops)

    B. Chieu Hoi Center operation

C. Exploitation

D. Resettlement (National Reconciliation)

A list of some of the activities:

    1. Psy-ops

    2. APT's – 1,000 men by the end of 1967.

    3. A province reception center in all 12 provinces (these can handle 22,500 people per year.

    4. A district office in all of those under GVN control.

    5. A Regional Center (will start construction in June, it can handle 4,800 people per year).

    6. Plans to build 17 resettlement hamlets.

    7. A very large program of coordination the exploitation of intelligence and psy-ops of Hoi Chanh.

    8. The task of providing employment for the Hoi Chanh.

    9. Monitoring the funding of the program in the Chieu Hoi Centers:

        a. Vocational training

        b. Education

        c. Agriculture

        d. Youth and sports

        e. Health and medical care

        f. Political training

        g. Self-help construction of facilities

        h. Self-defense (local security)

        i. Documentation of all records, the Bio-date, rallier card, ID, PR, etc.

        j. Housing and feeding of Hoi Chanh

The program to upgrade the Chieu Hoi Centers will continue and eventually all centers will meet the requirements.

    V Problems:

        A. Of primary concern to the Regional Advisor is the exploitation of the returnees. It would be desirable to "Task Force" the program at the regional level to effectively exploit the returnees to generate the intelligence and psy-ops to keep the program going. Exploitation by itself may not generate large numbers of returnees, but exploitation definitely enhances the success of military operations and these mil-itary operations in turn generate returnees. The "task force" would be made up of a representative of the agencies which could assist in the expedient use of intelligence and psy-ops. It is the opinion of the Regional Advisor that many of the problems of GVV/ARVN lack of interest in the Chieu Hoi Program would be overcome if they were to participate and receive the value of exploitation from the Chieu Hoi Program.

B. Funding of the program is still difficult but there has been some recent improvement in getting money to the province where it is needed. However, the normal bureaucratic method of finances inhibits the success of the program for psy-ops impact. The funding delays tend to discredit our own propaganda.

C. The lack of counterpart participation has required an "American takeover" in areas; this is not desirable. A greater emphasis should be placed on the GVN to generate greater Vietnamese participation in the program.

VI Conclusion:

A. If the 1966 estimates are correct, the cost per Hoi Chanh at $125.12 and approximately $340,000 to kill a VC, even though this is not a truly relative cost picture. The 3,500 lives of friendly forces which were saved in 1966, based on the kill ratio and number of returnees last year, the value of the program is established. These two facts taken together would give the Chieu Hoi Program a high prior-ity and assure the program the personnel and funds needed to be successful.

B. The Chieu Hoi Program is dependent upon military coordination and support and must react as rapidly as the military situation changes. The Chieu Hoi Program can be a proven program and have some predictability when its real value is recognized.

C. We have excellent IFFV cooperation and coordination with G-3 Psy-ops and G-2.

HEADQUARTERS
I FIELD FORCE VIETNAM
APO 96350

AVFA-CORDS-CHD   14 October 1967

MEMORANDUM FOR: IFFORCEV PSYOP Conferees

SUBJECT: IFFORCEV PSYOP Conference, 14 Oct 67

1. The periodic IFFORCEV PSYOP Conference will be held 141000H Oct 67 in the 5th Special Forces Group (Abn) conference room, Nha Trang. The agenda is as follows:

    1000   Convene. Opening remarks.

    1005   Discussion of agenda items.

    1130   Break for lunch. Lunch is available either in 5th SFGA Mess or Nha Trang Air Base QCM.

    1300   Reconvene. Continue discussion of agenda items.

    ----   Adjourn

2. Agenda items follow:

    a. IFFORCEV PSYOP Organization (Chieu Hoi Div).

    b. Coordination of PSYOP in II CTZ (Chieu Hoi Div).

    c. Improvement of thematic content of media against the NVA (Chieu Hoi Div).

    d. Status of province and district newspapers and radio broadcasting (PSYOP Div).

    e. Kit Carson Scout Program (Kontum Prov Rep).

    f. Leaflet dissemination training (Chieu Hoi Div.)

    g. New Equipment: Model 85 press set; 1000 watt loudspeaker set; logistics guide; etc (Chieu Hoi Div).

                                       RICHARD H. MERRITT, JR.
                                       Major, GS
                                       Chairman

BACKGROUND OF THE CHIEU HOI PROGRAM

Theory and National: Chieu Hoi, which translates into English as "Open Arms", is a defection program aimed at members and supporters of the Viet Cong, the so-called National Liberation Front, and elements of the North Vietnamese Army deployed in South Vietnam. Under this program the Government of the Republic of Vietnam provides an opportunity for insurgent elements to return to the National Just Cause and to become full-fledged citizens of the Republic. A defection program weakens the enemy forces by reducing their manpower, by impairing their morale, and by causing dissension and distrust in their ranks.

Origin and Results: The Chieu Hoi Program was adopted by the Government of Vietnam early in 1963, with advice and assistance from a number of United States organizations and individuals. It was based in part on experiences with defection programs in the Philippines, and in Malaya. As of 31 December 1966, a total of 48,041 members of the VC/NVA had come in to the Government under this program: 11,248 in 1963, 5,417 in 1964, 11,124 in 1965 and 20,242 in 1966. About two-thirds of these were arms-bearing VC, and it is estimated that bringing them in through Chieu Hoi way have saved the lives of some 3575 GVN/US soldiers. The total US/GVN cost of administering this program in 1966, exclusive only of salaries of U.S. personnel, was $ 125.12 per returnees.

Returnees: An individual returning to the GVN under the Chieu Hoi Program is known as a "Hoi Chanh", which translates simply as "returnee", with the connotation that the act of return was voluntary. A Hoi Chanh is any individual who, having given military or political support to the VC/NLF/NVA, voluntarily comes in and professes allegiance to the Government of the Republic of Vietnam. Male returnees are called "Anh Hoi Chanh", while female returnees are called "Chi Hoi Chanh". All are eligible for reception and care in a Chieu Hoi Center, for resettlement in South Vietnamese society, and for citizenship.

Objectives:

1. To induce military and civilian members of the VC/NLF/NVA to come over to the side of the GVN.
2. To obtain from the returnees information which is valuable for GVN/US intelligence and psychological operations purposes and to obtain their voluntary assistance in military tactical operations.
3. To weaken the Communist cause by causing a loss of military strength and civilian support; and at the same time to strengthen the GVN's cause.
4. To cause dissension and distrust among the communist military and political agencies.
5. To convert as many insurgents as possible into useful and contributing citizens of the Republic of Vietnam.

Some Salient Facts About the Chieu Hoi Program

In 1966, 20,242 Viet Cong returned voluntarily to the side of the GVN. Of these, 13,052 were armed, military Viet Cong. If it had been necessary to eliminate these Viet Cong by military means, the Free World forces would have lost approximately 3,000 dead, under prevailing kill ratios. Through the Chieu Hoi Program, the number of Viet Cong eliminated in 1966 was equal to one-third the number of all Viet Cong eliminated by all military forces in Vietnam - GVN, US, Free World combined. It should be noted, of course, that overall military pressure is a predominant factor in influencing the return of Viet Cong.

The cost of administering the Chieu Hoi Program in 1966 was $125.12 per returnee Viet Cong. This figure includes all US dollar and GVN piastre expenses for all aspects of the program excluding only staff salaries on the U.S. side.

The Target for 1967

The target is 45,000 Hoi Chanh. In 1966 we substantially doubled 1965 (20,242 versus 11,124). In 1967 we hope to more than double 1966. As of mid-February 1967 the returnee rate - projected over the whole year - is at the 30,000 plus level. And the VC who do come in are now being increasingly used against the enemy. We in Chieu Hoi are convinced that the ex-VC represent one of the great underestimated weapons for use in winning the war and saving lives on our side. This conviction is spreading throughout the US, Free World and GVN communities.

BLACKLIST CARD
3x5 White

V.C. AT LARGE	
Name :	Alias(s)
Age	Distinguished features
Position in V.C.	
Last known location-date	
Family information	
Additional remarks* Source of information* Date/place	

MẪU DANH THẺ LẬP CHO NHỮNG TÊN VIỆT CỘNG HÃY CÒN TẠI ĐÀO

VIỆT CỘNG TẠI ĐÀO	
Họ và tên	Bí danh & Bí số
Tuổi	Nhận dạng đặc biệt
Địa vị trong hàng ngũ V.C.	
Ngày và nơi có mặt lần chót	
Tin tức gia đình	
Cước chú, nguồn tin, ngày và nơi	

The blacklist card was an organizational tool used by Chieu Hoi to identify VC and NVA.

Safe conduct pass produced by Chieu Hoi. Anyone possessing this pass could safely defect and enter a Chieu Hoi Center. Millions of these leaflets were dropped all over South Vietnam to encourage VC to defect to Chieu Hoi.

Hoi Chanh gathered for roll call and inspection.

CHAPTER 7

TORTURE

Torture,1) the inflicting of severe pain to force information or confession, get revenge, etc. 2) any method by which such pain is inflected. 3) Any severe physical or mental pain; agony; anguish, physical discomfort.

Why would any self-respecting individual consent to administering physical or mental pain to another individual, then brag about it and claim to have used the most severe methods? This is not Psychological Operations. I saw results of torture, most of it not done in my presence; I would have prevented it. My education included human anatomy and physiology that provided me with an understanding of pain, nerve pain, and the critically sensitive points of the body. I stress this issue of torture because it has always been around in a sort of historical fog. But since Vietnam it became the United States of America's marker of our CIA- Military, as an acceptable treatment of suspects and POWs, often without any appearance of legal due process or compliance to our Constitution or international treaties. The French Foreign Legion in Algeria used fire and burned the subject's elbows, knees, and genitalia with a blow torch; these were third-degree burns. Then the subject was put in a cage where he could not straighten his arms and legs. After the burned flesh had congealed, the subject was taken out of the cage and his limbs were straightened out; this was excruciating pain. The subject usually begged for death, which was promised if he talked.

My experiences with torture took place in Vietnam in 1966-1968 and from reports it was increased considerably during years 1969-1972. Since then, especially during the recent George Bush Presidential period and after 9/11, as a tactic to counter-terrorism and gain military dominance over foreign indigenous populations with deployment of our military it has gained as acceptable. In fact, torture appears to have become an industry.

It now appears that some professional psychologists have found a new career path, that of mentoring our military on how to inflict sadistic pain and stress into interrogations of prisoners to obtain military intelligence. It is my opinion that the military will use any means necessary to justify their tactics such as torture, even to the point that it is done under the supervision of a trained military psychologist. To be selected and exposed to the pain of torture is a death sentence; there is no other way to erase the pain or its memory.

Before I get carried too far away from my personal resolve about torture in this writing, it is preposterous that any educated American who is younger than 65 years of age and has ridden the easy train of the gratuitous lifestyle that the Americans have had would involve themselves in any way with torture for any reason. There is no ambiguity in meaning; torture is torture. All those who apply it and those who sanction it are evil. Evil: 1a) morally bad or wrong; wicked, depraved. b) resulting from or based on conduct regarded as immoral. 2) causing pain or trouble; harmful; injurious. How far have we Americans allowed this country's leadership to sink in destroying this great nation?

I am not a psychologist; I am an American and proud of it, but of the last 30 years I have increasingly become ashamed to be part of a government that sanctions aggression, dominance, and torture to benefit but a few ambitious, greedy persons, or mentally unbalanced military officers. Why do I say this? It is because the military has a chain of command, what is at the bottom is the responsibility of the top.

There are things I observed that should not be made part of this record. War and the combat being seldom justified. Torture too often is used just for revenge. Of the many books written about the Vietnam War, most are critical of it and rightly so, but they place blame on the conduct of the military. There are other factors to blame, as much or more, like the CIA, USAID, The Joint Chiefs, and the White House. The Vietnam War was over more than 40 years ago and the same divisions of our government are worse every day. They are destroying this nation following the same faulted logic as The Headless Snake theory.

Why do I address the torture issue? Because I was there with the authority to act as I saw necessary to stop any activity counter to the instruc-tions I was given. Those simply were to achieve the maximum results from psychological field operations. I seldom visited the Provincial Interrogation Centers (PICS) because of my field contacts with enemy units. It must be understood that the VC had their agents everywhere, and my integrity as to fairness in defection (Chieu Hoi) and my Vietnamese agents would be compromised if I was connected to the Police Special Branch operation of the PICS. They were known widely for their torture by the Vietnamese community. The PIC buildings were found in all 44 provinces of Vietnam. They were built as a secure place to hold the enemy (assumed) to question and torture Vietnamese. They were actually run by the CIA (Americans) and Police Special Branch.

I had Police Special Branch ID and passes, but only used them looking for a particular POW for interrogation; someone whose interrogation report did not seem right and I wanted a shot at a better interrogation my way. I would take possession of them out of the PIC and take them to a Chieu Hoi facility. When I was seen entering a PIC, agents of my intelligence network warned that they were not going to continue working with me if I supported the PICS. Actually, some of my net worked for US, Army and Embassy, unbeknownst to the Americans.

In the field on psy-ops, I travelled totally independent of any specific organization for security other than my own, with the military as a General Staff Officer of IFFV, and the CIA via Air America. My access to reports and information was unlimited as a briefer of the Commanders Conference. The tales of some things in the field grew and were nothing but exaggerations;

these legends come with the veterans today. God Bless'em, true or false, they were there also.

"War college says the Army is filled with liars that need more firings," as displayed on the internet recently. This suggestion probably is applicable to the whole government and more. However, to the military, it is of importance. And it passed through my research for this book that the military was exploring interrogations of prisoners and the difficulty getting good intelligence. During the Vietnam War military interrogations were ineffective. The interrogation centers I oversaw were not abusing their prisoners and doing a good job, mostly at the Chieu Hoi Centers. American combat units, this was not always the case and we tried to stop things like putting lit cigarettes into the face of prisoners. Due to the rotation of American officers every six months, and the number of active units, it became difficult to stop some of the torture by unit intelligence officers, if only to consider the possible loss of intelligence from the prisoner.

It was difficult to understand torture when there was no personal threat to the officer using it. The loss of good enemy intelligence was unnecessary. We investigated several units on inquiries about prisoner torture. Of course, they answered from the combat units, "it was not us; it was them."

I have seen some of the worse torture and the results of torture, but nothing of the scale that has been recently published in the media (Guantanamo, Abu Ghraib). Torture is not part or parcel of Psychological Operations. The enemy used it as warfare inflicting pain to maintain control of people groups, not for information but to intimidate. The Phoenix Program used "black ops" for the same reason, and it was just as bad.

It is a fact that these actions of torture and intimidation have always failed their intended purpose to show cause; take note of Iraq, Afghanistan, Vietnam, and many undeclared wars or operations where we have sent our Killer Hunter personnel. Torture is wrong and should be forbidden for any American to commit...period. Torture is an illegal crime and those who use it should be prosecuted for its use severely. I believe that murder, rape, and torture should carry the death penalty as International Law, and no statute of limitation for the crime.

An agreement by all American organizations and individuals in any way associated with torture to announce the permanent and universal discontinued use of it in any form or method is essential to returning our behavior to a level of universal acceptance and national pride. Do it; most especially for *those Americans who have given all for our freedoms and liberties.*

PSYCHOLOGISTS AND TORTURE

Most people have a positive view of psychology as a profession of healing and explorers of the mind's mysteries, but the public's trust is not a given. It is earned and sustained by each member of the profession, from the therapist who helps someone overcome mental anguish to the researcher who conducts an ethical study of vulnerable populations. After 9/11, trust in the profession has been greatly damaged by the psychologists participating in the US torture program. Now, the public is learning about the British govern-ment's use of internet and how it can destroy reputations and lives. Moreover, GCHQ (Government Communications Headquarters) is showing the "online covert action" programs in its Human Science Operation Cell (HSOC) to agents in the National Security Association (NSA) and the other "Five Eyes" countries.

According to documents released by Edward Snowden, GCHQ trains people to use psychology as a weapon and this weapon is aimed at a broad range of communities. Agents infiltrate and exploit tensions within activist groups, make and spread false claims of abuse, and attempt to ruin friendships. Covert government smear campaigns are not new, of course, and the past century saw many innocent lives destroyed as a result. US history alone has seen such official campaigns used against Quaker pacifists, civil rights leaders, and labor organizers, among many others. No one should take comfort in assurances that the tactics will be aimed only at terrorists.

Nothing could be more contrary to a professional psychologist's ethical responsibilities than the destruction of a person's psyche, and few operations take the profession further from the Nuremberg Code for the protection of human research participants than GCHQ's HSOC program. Psychologists for

Social Responsibility calls on the British Psychological Society and the American Psychological Association to denounce the GCHQ covert action program and any other official program like it and declares that professional psychologists who are found to be involved in such programs risk disciplinary action for ethical transgression. Both organizations should explicitly ban pro-fessional psychologists from psy-ops research, development, and training which intends to bring harm to, cause suffering or otherwise damage human beings, or which carries a high risk of doing so.

The precursor to this article is a news article about a group of professional psychologists employed by the government to assist in the interrogation of other human beings as observers to certify that nothing immoral was in-volved; where it was public knowledge that waterboarding was used in the interrogations. To avoid a conflict the military declared that suffocating a per-son was not torture; well, it was unbelievable. That is until I started making inquiries into the profession and I am still caught off guard as to what I have discovered. In essence, the government wanted the profession (APA) to give up their code of ethics so the government can claim that POWs were not tortured because a licensed professional psychologist was in attendance. In 2012 I worked with Jean Maria Arrigo Ph.D., member of APA Divisions 19,26, and 48 on a report highlighting the military's use of psychologists' participa-tion in military sanctioned torture. She had been working for years to change the role of psychologists in the military from being complicit with torture to properly applying legal and ethical interrogation techniques. I contributed my experience in Vietnam as Psychological Operations Officer.

Let me make a point; in Vietnam, if I had found an American, *any* Ameri-can, assisting or instructing "waterboarding" or "electrical shock" in the man-ner used in the PICS they would have felt the authority I had to its fullness. At this point, I should inform you of the "legends" of war that develop from ru-mors or incidents and grow to become increasingly large facts retold as leg-end. It is human nature to exaggerate or attempt to duplicate, to build self-esteem, especially in areas of combat. As they would say in the field, be a "bad-ass, mean killer" as a good soldier. In my months in Vietnam, I covered the whole of South Vietnam with access to all classified daily situation reports of military and CIA. (I was not a CIA employee; I was assigned to work for the CIA). I have read books, stories, and military reports since the war that gave details of situations and conditions in an area where it just didn't happen or I would have been aware of or part of it. It sounds better if you make it appear to be worse; this makes the legend and reputation greater. The overreaction to some of these legends just made them worse as word is circulated; the worse the legend claimed, the faster and wider the attempt to duplicate the atrocity or brutality such as torture. I was assigned by the Embassy to investi-gate and stop, by any means necessary, these acts or legends to prevent them from spreading within American military units. And I did, again developed a routine (psychology) to convince the troops I was there to put a stop to them.

Killing is a way of life in war, as for body counts, any body will do; when invading a foreign country, it is impossible to determine his or her allegiance by sight, and dead people don't tell.

There is no justification for torture and those who support it are guilty of the most heinous crime a person can perform; just remember that your conduct can be no greater than your opponents because they normally will retaliate with more or greater of the same. How do those who are employed by the military in some capacity to develop means obtain essential information from insurgents or enemies via physical or mental stress; you are a criminal by international law or treaty, if not by lack of common sense.

Let me give you a couple of facts from Vietnam that I am sure apply to Iraq and Afghanistan.

With the increasing use of Hunter-Killer teams and assassinations, surges, and drones, the military can report many apparent successes via numbers; what the military doesn't see is that the population is aware of the fact that an invader is killing countrymen who dare to oppose the invader. And this invader-occupier considered collateral deaths of non-insurgent family members as acceptable conduct. With this killing and torture, you are strengthening the indigenous population resolve to continue to resist. I reviewed a video on my computer of what looked like bunches of dirty laundry getting into a small pick-up. In reality, it was Taliban, seven of them crammed into the truck holding their AK47 rifles firmly in hand; their bearded faces showed determination. They were going someplace to kick some invader butts. They were going without tanks, cannons, airplanes; but they were going to defend their culture and families. What has the military invader (USA) been defending? A corrupt government or a highly profitable drug trade to profit from.

The 1968 Tet enemy offensive in Vietnam, it caught the US military off guard and was a blow politically for the US. But to cover it up, the US stressed the point that the enemy suffered massive losses, which they did, mostly Viet Cong (South Vietnamese). I was sent to the countryside to get an estimate of the number of enemy VC killed. What I found of the 35,000 reported killed by the White House, 15,000 were civilians caught in the wrong place at the wrong time, and another 20,000 were South or North Vietnamese possible enemy. The enemy military dead was difficult to obtain because the Americans did not, as government policy, register Asian dead because they were considered "subhuman." During this assignment, I wrote a memo to the CIA trying to stop their propaganda of how we killed massive numbers of the enemy during Tet, which would be great news for the people back home. The other side to this I tried to counteract or create a different view psychologi-cally with my resources that with the impact of Tet, the population saw Viet-namese taking the fight to the invader (American military). My effort was to portray the VC as agents of the North to enslave the South. It appears I was to be the only American who attempted to make this point with my fellow Americans. To continue to stress so loudly and often the "massive enemy losses" was a victory for the "American" war effort did not sit well with many South Vietnamese.

But the American population called for quits in Vietnam; the enemy Tet offensive killed what support the American public had for the war.

After Tet '68, the Phoenix Program became the methodology directed by the CIA to fight the war. The US made attempts at pacification with limited success. Tactics changed and the effort to seek and kill VC leaders increased. To define targets (assumed to be leaders of the VC) they needed intelligence, thus torture became the essential intelligence-gathering method. Once they had a "possible name," they killed whomever without any real evidence. All of this, plus the change of attitude of the population, they kept in the shadows for fear of being tortured and killed as a suspect. The US really misread the common indigenous population minds to think that US bullets can solve everybody's problems for the betterment of the people. Check our success rate; we spent trillions, lost thousands of our military, and still using the same methods. Name one success.

Stop and think, if our philosophy is reflected in our Constitution it would seem to me that our society should have made us the most envied nation on earth, not the most feared.

I look at psychology as the medium which supports and allows all societies to function; it must have a code of ethical behavior to prevent wildcat schemes from taking advantage of our society.

Society is built around the family; it is a natural occurrence. War tends to destroy families, in fact, the family becomes a target as a tool to enforce control; think of the military draft.

Knowing and accepting cultural differences is not a defeatist position; it is the initial step toward a mutual understanding between divergent societies.

The appearance of men in uniforms with guns has a history based on fear and not of cooperation and compassion.

Persuasion with Relevance is my psychological war strategy developed in the field in Vietnam to reduce the loss of life and property; it does not deny the use of force if rightly needed.

Military dominance as invasion and or occupancy supported by such things as torture and drone attacks will eventually fail to bring a victory, regardless of whoever claims it. If that is the objective, it will only bring resentment and generations of hate.

The Vietnam War was fought with up to 500,000 in the country, and 200,000 in support. By July 1968, it was recognized as a lost cause and the change in tactics as described as "cut the head off the snake, it will die;" which in reality only applies to snakes. So, Phoenix was the chosen vehicle to kill VC, infrastructure, and shadow government leaders. Quotas were set for the mil-itary; the goal was 1,800 per month and scores were kept. So, to be success-ful, the higher the body count the better, anyone's body.

I disagreed because my methods were doing better with the development of Persuasion with Relevance strategy. They, the military since Vietnam, came up with the concept of counterinsurgency warfare, known as COIN, for the tactic of choice in Iraq and Afghanistan; it has failed. The reason being it was basically a Phoenix program dressed up as a full military strategy. It is unbelievable as it failed to produce the necessary results with a new approach. It failed because it was used as a tactic along with other conven-tional systems. They recognized the need to relate to the people, and HTT was created; the Human Terrain Team, composed of professional psychologists in military uniforms and paraded through Afghanistan to gain a cultural understanding of the Afghans. I read the idea was abandoned after a few anthropologists were killed.

And now I find that the military has psychologists on the military payrolls as advisors on proper interrogation and torture methods. Unbelievable. It is noted that they are also trying to reduce the number of suicides of US military.

They, the military, just don't understand persuasion via a psychological strategy can get favorable results without torture and killing civilians; or maybe they do understand but are trained to be sadistic in their approaches to war. Persuasion isn't all things for all purposes but is adaptable.

Recap:
- I got involved in this debate with professional psychologists because I developed alternative strategies to reduce causalities by deploying military differently when and where applicable.
- It is my opinion that the disadvantages of using torture outweigh any advantages as far as intelligence gained.
- It is of concern that American military captured would be exposed to torture because we deemed it as an acceptable tactic of our war efforts. Is there a limit to the nature or degree of pain we think is an approved method? How sadistic a method is acceptable?
- War the way we fight it is frightening; our apparent disregard for human life, and our seemly refusal to prosecute the individuals when the killing of those civilians without sufficient proof that they are

enemy is barbaric. In civilized countries, this is considered as murder without cause.

- There are types of intelligence typically of interest in military deployment; in the occupancy phase, there are further elements needed.

Again, the legends of war must be taken with the knowledge that they may not be what they seem. Torture in any form or to any degree is wrong and only in rare circumstances would the results be of military importance.

By trying to accomplish our military missions and responsibilities by the use of irregular techniques by claiming results that warrant any extreme is a product only from the minds of criminal, sadistic people.

How many thousands of troops and material do we have on foreign soil claiming to fight terrorism? We get an occasional report that a drone blew up a school or wedding party, etc.

We really are kept uninformed and the military costs keep increasing; suicides in the ranks of our military are now exceeding our combat deaths. We are killing people in places most Congressmen can't pronounce.

In the war against the threat of nonstate terrorists, what is the cost benefits of Gitmo? Is it not just another way to suck money out of the treasury for a few CIA-military with a failed intelligence scheme? I had some experience with torture as mostly the results afterward, considerable experience with interrogation and intelligence gathering, enough to know the limits and the better methods.

MY VIEW OF THE VIETNAM WAR OF INTERROGATIONS WITH TORTURE

The subject of interrogations and torture used by the American govern-ment is not easily understood by people because they have never been exposed to it as a government program. It has only been exposed as being "over there somewhere." Yes, torture has quite a history; military interroga-tion and torture have appeared in stories and movies over the years with only a hint that it was used in recent years as an American policy. The mainstream media has not been showing the application of stress or pain applied to living humans undergoing interrogation by our military-CIA. So, generally most people have only some vague idea of it but no contact with it as Americans traditionally treat such things; it is someone else's problem.

I had observed in Vietnam various methods of torture before, during, and after it was used to heighten the results of interrogations on prisoners or suspects. Let's understand that if you are tortured you are a prisoner by the very fact of being restrained against your will. Whether a prisoner of war (POW) or not, the idea of a uniform or not, this is not the relevant point. The rules of engagement and international treaties and law are the determining factors. This phony idea that you are suspect and therefore have no rights is a play on words, and a stretch at that, not reality. During torture, tell me what the difference is between suspect and prisoner; show me the difference. There is none; so, to restrict a person to torture makes for a prisoner with certain rights by treaty; if not law, then inalienable human rights. Anything less would be plain savagery.

Those among us who follow this ridiculous concept that torture is an acceptable method of psychological interrogation to be used on suspects are themselves savages and should display themselves as savages and be treated as such. There is no grey area to debate about this; torture is a crime. I used the word savage as to mean without civilization, primitive.

Some people (Military-CIA) apparently have a sadistic logic in their character make up and accept the theory that torture has a use in finding out "critical information" (intelligence) of such value it justifies torture by any means on human beings. Another failed logic, an excuse to use torture. Reasoning questions why any situation would have deteriorated to a point where the last invasive report is to torture unreliable suspects in a vain effort to obtain critical information. You can assume if the torture was reversed and put on the torturer they would be screaming bloody murder that it was illegal and criminal. May I suggest that as long as the American government con-dones and utilizes it, it seems the only humane thing to do is to at random, select from our government torturers a few representatives and put them to their torture methods to certify that it is sufficiently painful for use in getting intelligence information. We really do not have a certifiable answer about this.

Simply put torture is used as a means to find a solution desired by one against one or more other unaligned desires. I use the word "desires" because it could represent a material or mental objective. In today's complex world we can desire materials such as oil, gold, land, etc. or as mentally the enslave-ment of populations by denying freedoms. In our case, America and our allies, it appears to be both. Although, in our situation as Americans we should be guided by our unique, as far as human history goes, Declaration of Independence and Constitution. But the expedient use of a play on words has been condoning torture as a means of determining truth; it has reduced our society to that of savagery. Where philosophy is the study of reasoning and logic, psychology is the medium in which our society functions, at least that is the way I understand it. Beyond that, we are either created or evolved to survive and reproduce and that is it. I think therefore I am. To trample our inalienable rights as a feasible means to satisfy military desires is contrary to our American rights in pursuit of happiness.

THERE IS NO JUSTIFICATION FOR USING TORTURE

My experience with interrogations by torture was in Vietnam, and my exposure to it increased as my exposure to the culture of the CIA increased. While I began to become exposed to the American government's modus operandi as an invading dominant force in Vietnam, with torture and Search and Destroy tactics, the more it became counterproductive to the Chieu Hoi and psychological field operations I was developing using psychological (Persuasion with Relevance) means to influence population without violence.

How can your promises be kept of returning to a peaceful life if you defect from the Viet Cong (enemy) via the Chieu Hoi program, if you continue to hear or see killing and torturing of family members from their village resulting from military Search and Destroy Killing Teams? The government (Vietnamese-CIA) even went so far as to build a torture chamber (a large, free-standing building) in all 44 provinces in the country. Such was a monument to incompetence, the failure to understand the local society and display in any sense even the smallest understanding of "human decency."

As you will find in other sections of this book, the interrogation methods I used successfully were outside of the famed Provincial Interrogation Centers (PICS). Due to my Chieu Hoi involvement, I had made very good connections with many Vietnamese and had established five intelligence agent nets with very strong mutual integrity and confidence within them. It was suggested to me that I should avoid contact with the PICS, the appearance of which could be considered as a threat to my Vietnamese associates (agents and contacts) due to the reputation of the PICS.

Methods to obtain results from interrogations took planning and surveying the possible POWs to find good sources. It appeared to me, that as a result of an American sweep of an enemy area, the push in interrogating was for tactical data. Most prisoners were banged around in the attempt to get the tactical data (enemy unit size, location, and arms, etc.). In the VC and NVA, only senior officers were aware of any future plans and those officers were not often captured. The VC-NVA used a "closed cell" manpower for security; it was comprised of three members. Each was accountable for each other, and if one defected, the other two were shot and the current planning or operation changed to defeat any intelligence of their plans.

A week or two later when the interrogation reports were coming in, I would scan for injured POWs, local business owners, and/or educated members with community connections with an accessible family. I would visit the family, ask if they had letters for the prisoner and I would give to him the next day, and take a picture of them for him. I would ask if they were ok considering the circumstances. Note, I was not in uniform and was accompa-nied by two former VC Chieu Hoi from this same area.

At POW compounds, I had a routine Fly in an Air America helicopter (not military), land near the compound. My interpreter and I got out and walked into the compound like we owned it. Borrow the Commandant's office and walk out through the compound to locate our POW. We were not in anything that would suggest we were military. Find our man, greet him, shake hands and walk with him back to the office. Give him the letters and picture and any verbal messages. Then give him pen and paper to write a letter to his family while the Commandant brought us tea. I told him why I was in Vietnam and about my family. I stressed that I was there to settle things and stop the fighting the best way possible. In the 45 minutes, I never asked him a direct tactical question I would check up on his health and be back in three days. I had him seal the envelope letter to his wife, and I walked him back into the compound. Three days later, the same routine, only he asked for more paper and pen, which we supplied. He then gave us three contact points in his com-munity and two arms cache locations and wrote another letter to his wife, which he sealed. We delivered; she read and said thanks and it instructed her to give us more information. When we walked him back into the compound this time, he introduced us to eight other POWs. I followed up with Chieu Hoi and had them go and talk to him and the other eight and to make a low-key visit to his wife; they got more names.

I did this scenario seven different times and scored big each time. Average time from capture to my last visit six weeks, but it does pay off. I never asked him for intelligence information.

It is creating the right image the right way...

There is more; it is what training the Team is about.

I have reviewed information on torture, to permit torture is criminal.

Most prisoners taken are physically abused in the process, some more than others who resist. My personal view on this is in a hot combat exchange a prisoner is more of an intelligence asset than a dead enemy. I also believe he who shoots first gets to live longer. It is war, and there are risks as we fight. We then sometimes rush too quickly into combat due to lack of purpose other than body count, strategy and firepower. Agreed, in some circumstances fire-power is required, no doubt. But good timing and planning are too.

I have seen torture in the PICS and none was applied by Americans; it was always by Vietnamese. Water Boarding was not that apparent, electric shock was. And as it was applied, that's open to debate. The method was to put a bamboo under the subject's knees and then his elbows under the same pole and strap the subject into a fetal position, then apply electric shock. The brain gets the message of pain and tells the body *get me out of here*; the body can't. The large action muscles are restricted and the brain, if treated to too much, can be seriously damaged where it loses all bodily functions and eventually leads to death.

Also, from experience, the recent description of the CIA waterboarding is questionable. Waterboarding is the most common form used by Americans because it does not mark or leave wounds. The method they are using is incomplete; the subject must strive to have eye contact with the questioner. Waterboarding is descriptive of using a teeterboard contrivance with again the body unable to react, strapped to the board so the brain signals, *get us out of here; we are drowning*. The eye contact communication is the psychological factor essential in the process. If properly administered, it would be uncommon for a subject to survive three treatments.

There are other very extreme methods used on principal subjects withholding vital information. I have never witnessed, but I have observed the results on the victim. I have never authorized any torture. Some I happened to encounter, on review of their records, would not have been taken as a prisoner to begin with as to circumstances.

ONCE YOU START TORTURING YOU ARE IN DANGER THAT IT WILL BE RECIPROCATED.

We used other, more intelligent techniques when operating in the field to gain information as part of the Spear Team; we developed an interrogation environment by staging the proper surroundings. We psychologically conditioned the POW by lessening the threat rather than increasing it, as is most commonly used by most.

I assume it is now safe to describe another method we employed secretly to get good interrogation prospects. When a large sweep of an area to apprehend VC-NVA was in process we would watch as they assembled the detainees in a holding area and pick out the better prospects for interrogation our way. I trained several Vietnamese government Chieu Hoi Program members by sharpening their body language knowledge to identify NVA and VC leaders within the POW preliminary holding area. We sent in and offered our prospect Chieu Hoi rather than POW. We never failed to score big. No one ever knew what we were doing.

The American military faced a defeat in Vietnam and as with several wars since then they have lost, yet still think they have the answers to defeat any small country that they attack. The most recent ones were initiated by attempts at killing or deposing of the foreign country's leadership with Hunter-Killer Special Forces and foreign mercenaries, based partially on intel-ligence from the torture of suspects identified as terrorists. This is where the Americans have come to today. The recent rapid increase of the Special Operations teams in our military and the deployment of them outside of the United States, along with increasing numbers of drones, all speak to the fact that the United States has possibly become history's largest active terrorist nation.

The increasing demand for "suspects" aimed at gaining needed intelli-gence to operate these Special Operations killer teams (they are not Peace Corps) and the military's failed ability to successfully exploit required intelli-gence gathering efforts to begin with have facilitated interrogation torture to distract from the fact that their human field intelligence was lacking. Thus, the military-CIA stating that abusive interrogation will produce required intel-ligence. Don't believe it; good intelligence is very time perishable and the enemy uses a "closed cell" manpower for security.

Psychologists, I did not know if there were any in South Vietnam when I was there, other than the army trained psychological warfare operations (psy-ops) personnel. Psy-ops is not to be confused with Special Operations-Hunter-Killer Teams.

I was assigned to develop Psychological Operations that initially centered on the Chieu Hoi Program. Upon on my arrival in II Corps, Chieu Hoi was in a state of confusion, corruption, mismanagement, and lacked integrity of pur-pose. I suppose that is why the Embassy assigned it to me on arrival in Vietnam. Where was I trained in psy-ops? In the field and Chieu Hoi com-pounds where there were hundreds of VC who had defected from the VC. In Binh Dinh Province, the compound was the largest in the Vietnam population-wise but totally lacked adequate facilities. So, my deputy and I with two Filipino contract employees started to build and build...we worked daily with the compound occupants (it was a secured compound with guards) building dor-mitories, kitchen and mess hall, numerous classrooms and shops. We had a 90-hole outdoor facility and a soccer field.

Again, we took the time to learn about the Vietnamese and they, in turn, made every effort to get to know us as a few non-belligerent, body counting American civilians. And there is evidence that this reputation spread among the Vietnamese. It paid many dividends in our future work with the Vietnamese.

Chieu Hoi at work clearing the ground surrounding the compound.

Our American military policy today is the antithesis of nonviolent persuasion with their body counts and military dominance by any means (surges, counterinsurgencies, and drones). The American good neighbor policy of choice is our military, that in my opinion creates more anti-American terrorists than they can find to torture and kill. Stupid is as stupid does. Yes, there are many situations that require force, but making force the initial primary solution is wrong; study the alternatives first.

The Headless Snake admonishes the military for its lack of leadership and failure to reform their strategy. Not to be misunderstood, I support the men and women in our military and I am forever in their debt for their service and sacrifice for this nation. I worked with a few outstanding military and CIA in-dividuals in Vietnam.

A NOTE OF CAUTION

The torture for gaining intelligence is one thing that uses inflicting pain as a method of interrogation to obtain needed intelligence, assuming the suspect or POW has the intelligence they need, which is an unknown to the interrogator.

The pain used to intimidate the population is generally not thought as torture but an act of war, and it is not necessarily limited to a one-on-one situation, but via napalm, drone, cluster bombs, carpet bombing, and Hunter Killer Teams against undefended civilian populations. All of these are counter to any idea of ever obtaining a peaceful settlement. The collateral loss of life of noncombatants is an act of savagery.

American military policy (currently supported by the American popula-tion) seems to be determined to become the world's leader in terrorism, intimidation, and continual war upon their military objectives as well as civilians.

How did we get to this point? Of recent note, our American Department of Justice indicates it will not prosecute those government officials who use torture, even those who torture suspects to death. This is really bad public relations at its worse. I don't remember the lecture in, "How to win and influence people" using torture as a means.

In the field work, human intelligence, (HUMINT) is carefully developed without having to overcome the current savagery we throw at indigenous populations via drones and non-state empowered mercenaries with their atrocities. If our cause is just; then torture is not needed. *Period*. Those who order it or condone it are guilty of a capital crime of international law.

As an afterthought, I wonder how soon the Pentagon and Department of Justice will be ordering the "Approved Rack" based on the design of the rack that was so successful during the Inquisition. This government model has been endorsed by CIA and Military Intelligence.

Good military intelligence and properly trained interrogators do not need torture. In my field missions to develop Psychological Operations for the Phoenix Program, we found ways to accomplish good interrogations that were producing five times the intelligence as the PICS.

THE ZERO-SUM GAME OF TORTURE

I guess it is possible that in the 237 years since 1776 the population of America could evolve a primitive morality in the same society that created the Constitution and Bill of Rights. In fact, they have, and have declared torture is not immoral or a crime. In fact, they made torture a government official policy.

In my desire to advance the concept of Psychological Operations to reduce the needless destruction of life and property that has become the image of our American military aggressive adventurism in the world today, I developed Persuasion with Relevance, a psychological strategy. With my experience in the Vietnam War as a basis to work from, I began researching the military's grand development of "counterinsurgency" (COIN), as their strategy for future wars that was ideally created but improperly organized and deployed; and it failed. This book, *The Headless Snake,* is my effort to reconstruct Psychological Operations as the primary alternative to COIN and all the other useless destructive tactics of war.

In my research, I recently came across unbelievable information about the use of torture as a logical means of gaining intelligence from "suspects." It is supervised by American professional psychologists employed by the American government to instruct and supervise interrogations and torture. Again, unbelievable.

Vietnam was two generations of military history ago; it was our first major war fought against a civilian light infantry, gorilla style army. Lessons learned?

Not really, but as a precursor to the future, Vietnam has been rewritten to promote and support changes in our current military. To understand the military American-style you must deal with numbers; they like their successes dramatized with numbers like enemy killed, land areas secured, number of bombs, and more recently, leaders killed. This point connects us to the issue of torture.

My personal interests are in developing the Persuasion with Relevance in order to restrict the need to murder or torture "suspects" as an ordinary military tactic in the attempt to inflict total dominance on an enemy or a whole country. There is ample evidence that the United States of America has murdered millions of people who were not aligned with any group that threatened the United States. The Persuasion with Relevance strategy incorporates psychological training to help and coordinate the resolving of insurgent problems by being a positive example and not the evil invader and torture chamber operators. After a lot of field time in Vietnam, I learned that the psychological approach to populations can be very productive and bene-ficial by reducing the loss of life, theirs and ours. And yes, there will be at different locations and cultures, resistance fomenting violence but there are methods to overcome them without attacking everybody, especially those who are not directly involved.

Our current military threats seem to be directed toward those countries that are now, or in the future, potentially a threat to our international corporations and banks more than to our national security. Here in such situations, a negotiated joint cooperative agreement would be better and much less expensive than military tactics we frequently rely on now. We must emphasize that everything the Department of Defense does is an expense piled onto the backs of the taxpayers. Generally, the military conduct has killed and destroyed numerous former allies and produced no friends. We must become less aggressive and shift our military strength into serving nations in need, by offering a true heart of compassion in times of stress instead of bombing them. Yes, it is a complex world and there are bad people, but their numbers are far less than those who we can influence as friends rather than foes. We must change directions because we cannot sustain our sovereignty by the behavior we now seem to promote. Our position among the nations of the world should (and to survive as free people) be one of greatness demonstrated by aiding with hospital ships and emergency supplies rather than drones with bombs and our torture chambers.

Recap:
- Torture is inhumane and must stop; we are not savages.
- Denying a person liberty makes a prisoner, not a suspect; it's the law.
- A helping hand is more often accepted than a hand with gun or bomb.
- To those who persist in attacking us, we should use our skills to neutralize all of their support base with Persuasion with Relevance instead of aggressive dominance
- The United States of America should be demonstrating its power for peace rather than its military arsenals for war and dominance.

CHAPTER 8

EVENTS

These stories are events and opportunities that occurred where I happened to be at the time and were, for the most part, in addition to my normally heavy schedule with Chieu Hoi, Psychological Operations, Special Assignments, and staff duties with Military Intelligence.

The Vietnamese nicknamed me Nụ cười (Smile).

All were based on my personal relationships and concern for the plight of the Vietnamese population. In matters of warfare, knowledge and experience comes from being in the field where there is activity dealing with problems and people. (The Air We Breathe). With all my activities, I gave credit where credit was due.

I think my success came from being able to cross over the various government organization lines of authority without being a threat to their positions.

BUFFALO SACRIFICE

There was a celebration planned for the return of the Mnong Tribe out of Cambodia to their Province by sacrificing a water buffalo and campfire (you could say "dance" but that might be a little misleading under the circum-stances). This took place somewhere in the jungle on the Vietnamese–Cam-bodian border area, mostly an uncivilized area.

Members of the Mnong Tribe. Chief M'Bloi Eban is wearing sunglasses.

If I remember, the tribe had about 30 members in their camp, the Vietnamese Province Chief who provided the buffalo, me and the local CIA representative (his story was very interesting). The tribe members constructed a very decorative altar out of logs to which the buffalo tethered. The party began by M'Bloi Eban, the Mnong Chief, chanting a few prayers to the "Spirit" that will soon receive this buffalo. It is an occasion by sound and sight you never forget. As the sacrifice began a "Spirit Man" came out with a large ax and whacked the buffalo's rear legs' tendons and the buffalo went down; then the front legs were done the same. The sound of the ax hitting tendon and bone was very discomforting for me. Now I was thinking *what else could they do to this poor animal* and here was that man again, this time with a big metal spear which he jammed into the side of the buffalo, into the heart. He controlled the flow of blood by how he held the spear. He definitely appeared to know what he was doing. Then they began collecting the blood in quart jars, filling them about half full. The CIA man and I were looking at each other. *What is this for*? We found out they mixed it with their homebrew rice beer. You guessed it; we were the guests of honor so we got to drink the first toast to the Tribe. I carefully got one swallow down and said thanks. So, they brought me a quart of their homebrew; that wasn't much of an improvement.

After everyone had a quart or two of homebrew the feast began. I was provided a plate of food, some part of that poor buffalo. I took a chance and ventured a bite; the taste was ok, but it did not chew. So, I found out it was the buffalo's stomach, which is eaten first because the other meat takes longer to cook. Then this old Chief started telling us about the Catholic priest they cooked and ate back in the early 1950's, (apparently it is true). He said that the hands were very tender and best part.

It was getting dark, so the fire was stoked up and the band began to play. The band, two snare drums, a one string screech fiddle, and finger cymbals on the ladies' fingers, began to play and most everybody was feeling no pain. The ladies, old and young, begin to dance around the fire, something between a "temple dance" and a "sensual dance." Yes, of course, the CIA and I were invited to join the dance.

Now, can you tell me how many people in the world have been guests of honor at a buffalo sacrifice, ate part of the buffalo for supper, drank blood and homebrew, and danced the night away with a tribe of former cannibals? And shared all of this with a CIA covert agent out of Europe.

Their history notwithstanding, I found them as wonderful friends and survivors. I loved each and every one of them.

The young (early 30's) CIA person who shared this adventure with me was mad at the world and the CIA. His story was that he had been recruited while in college; he spoke a European language with the correct accent (his family's language) and had been put into a European country as a covert agent. Over six or seven years he had a full-time job, a close relationship with a girl and was well accepted in this country. He had been abruptly called back to Wash-ington and assigned to duty in Vietnam...his life to that point down the drain and his identity destroyed for good. His career derailed, all to be sitting in a remote part of the world doing nothing.

Of the many nights I spent in CIA safe houses around the country, his story was often heard from others. Those night time conversations were very interesting to hear. A once in a lifetime event of such a gathering of special intelligence agents from all over the world, meeting informally and being free to talk about their lives could only happen at that time.

You will find in this section of events more information on the Mnong Chief. I think this relationship illustrates my theory of "The Air We Breathe" from the close contact required for field operations.

The two days William Colby gave me to clear post I was told an NVA company had entered the Mnong village. So, the Air Force napalmed the village, no survivors of the 130 Mnong. Years past after news of Colby's sudden death, I have heard from other agents he was assassinated.

Most of the books written have a basis on second-hand knowledge, from participants who were MACV at sub-sector or sector posts. Not to belittle them, but they are limited in overall experience and scope of activities.

Success comes from the good intelligence of the mission and the people skills that produce the chemistry between you and "them." No amount of in-struction and theorizing can overcome lack of attitude.

CONDENSED MILK

One of the best intelligence nets in all of Vietnam and it was supported by condensed milk.

Vietnam had no dairy farms, and the stores did not sell milk. The American commissary in Cholon (Saigon) sold canned milk.

One night at my villa in Nha Trang there was a pounding on the door. There stood a very beautiful Vietnamese lady; she spoke no English but sounded like she was in distress So, I let her in, got her to sit down and gave her water. I went to get an interpreter.

The story, in brief, she was the number one Madam for prostitution in the Nha Trang area and had delivered a baby in my villa 20 months earlier when it was occupied by an American doctor. She had been released after one year from prison three days earlier in Phan Rang, a three-day walk south of Nha Trang. She needed help; if she was caught they would execute her for prosti-tution My next-door neighbor was the head jailer for the Province. I got him; he knew her and said she was a nice person. Apparently, her arrest had more to do with the criminal rackets than her trade.

At 2 AM what do I do? The jailer said to let her stay for a day to rest up, and he would find out what was happening about her. Daylight and my inter-preter arrived, and we heard the most unusual story of prostitution and crime in Vietnam. The jailer reported that a criminal gang was looking for her, some-thing about kickback money they wanted from her. The jailer said she needed to be protected for a while. I knew the Vietnamese Airborne Rangers had a big house they ran; would she be safe there? I got an American doctor to check her out, and she was ok.

The Vietnamese Airborne Rangers' house of prostitution was a four-story apartment building of 32 units guarded by a detachment of Rangers; this was where the girls lived but worked outside My presence made the guards upset and aggressive until my passenger spoke and then their attitudes totally changed. By then we were attracting a crowd of girls, some with young babies and my passenger introduced me as a friend.

"What else can I do?" I asked.

"*MILK*, we need milk so we can go back to work."

So, every trip to Saigon I bought a case of "Old Miners" condensed milk at the commissary.

For being considerate and a friend, I had just tied into one of the best intelligence nets in all of Vietnam, not just the girls, but the Rangers who had connections in everything. They operated totally outside of American involve-ment. Tips from the girls possibly saved my life several times. It should be noted I did not share my contacts with anyone, obviously for security reasons. They did warn me of the 1968 Tet attacks a week in advance, and I brought all my staff into safe locations out of the field. I reported the information through channels; MACV didn't pay attention. Give help freely; you never know how you might be repaid.

CORRUPTION IN BINH DINH

One night I was called into the Embassy at 10:00 PM for a meeting with Wilfred Koplowetz, a CIA agent, and Lewis Lapham, Deputy Ambassador. To my surprise, they recommended I get out of the country for a few weeks because they were of the opinion my life was threatened. How did they know and why?

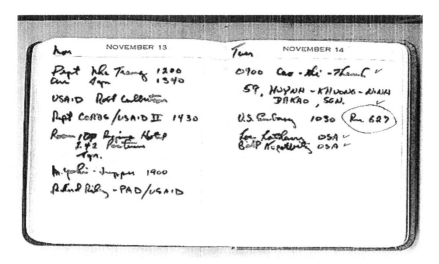

My diary entry noting late-night meeting at the US Embassy with Koplowetz and Lapham.

The US government had been building a case against a senior US Naval officer (head of ports) and a Vietnamese woman who was running one of the largest black-market schemes in the country at that time. They were suspected of stealing everything of value directly from ships under the control of a naval officer. Military Intelligence could not get proof because they could not get into the private property (warehouses) owned by a Vietnamese family with high government connections.

This corruption reached the Province Chief of Binh Dinh Province. My involvement began at the Chieu Hoi Center and the theft of supplies that never made it to the Center but could be found on the black market. I knew the Chieu Hoi Chief was dealing in the black market, and I had warned him about it. However, he had good high-level associations within the Regional Military through his wife's family. So, on this trip, I got a truck and crew of returnees. We went looking for our material, and we hit it pretty good. In the process, one of the Hoi Chanh told us the location of some warehouses where he had helped take stolen materials from the Center. Off we went to the warehouses. We found there were five or six metal buildings, all with armed security guards. The returnee pointed out the buildings where they had unloaded stolen material.

This is the scenario, a Vietnamese government truck with six Chieu Hoi returnees and an American not in uniform, but with a black leather holster with a large caliber pistol confronting the armed guards and telling them to step aside as the American breaks into the warehouses. The buildings were filled to capacity with contraband materials and PX supplies of all types, cigarettes, rice, etc. We loaded up the Chieu Hoi material and departed; I noticed a crowd gathering as we left.

It seems that some honest public citizens decided to prosecute in this situation as an attack against government black marketing. I, however, had no further contact with it. There was a rumor the Province Chieu Hoi Chief was killed.

The Province Chief of Binh Dinh was hung and his two bodyguards were shot. This Province Chief was the most decorated officer in the Vietnamese Army; I got along with him, and he was a fine officer. In my opinion, he did own the buildings, but the black-market was run by a General's wife (sister-in-law of the Chieu Hoi Province Chief) with the cooperation of a US Naval Admiral, not the Province Chief.

This was the first major corruption prosecution of the war. Results, the Navy Admiral was dishonorably discharged, all pensions and pay suspended.

The Vietnamese report that we received was a typical "whitewash" investigation made by the Vietnamese based on a request I had made over the loss of medical supplies at the Chieu Hoi Center.

The Embassy was concerned that the corrupt organizations within the Vietnamese government (and there were many of them) would take this opportunity to kill me as a warning to keep Americans out of what they considered their private business. The CIA wanted me to leave the country for safety until Military Intelligence could get more information. I told them I would not leave. I am lucky to be alive and probably only because I had good friends in the highest Vietnamese power structure.

M'Bloi Eban

M'Bloi Eban was the young chief of the Mnong Tribe of Montagnards; they were the first tribe to capture and hold a province capital in the Fulro move-ment in 1965 in South Vietnam. They came into Gia Nghia, probably the least developed province in the country of Vietnam; they had been held by the north as slaves in an old French base camp in Cambodia.

I listed them as refugees and not Chieu Hoi to support them. It seemed the USAID (CORDS) Regional Director did not want more refugees on his record. I made them Chieu Hoi, and with support from the Commander of Special Forces (Col Ladd) was able to provide weapons, uniforms, food, and medical assistance. I arranged for a civilian American doctor to check them out for illnesses.

M'bloi, with two wives and boy child, came to Nha Trang to live with me; we didn't know about the second wife in our planning. Later, I went to live with them during construction of their village while carrying out my other regional duties. His older wife was a real queen; she was very intelligent and so poised, quite a lady to come from an environment so poor. She earned my total respect. We put M'bloi to work in psy-ops to help us bring other Monta-gnards into the government side. Before this was completed, I was trans-ferred to Saigon and the Phoenix Program.

The old men of the tribe tell stories around a campfire about the past; this tribe was, as reported, the last cannibals in Indochina. As recent as 1950's, they cooked a Vietnamese Catholic priest; the Montagnards did not like the Vietnamese who exploited them for years as sub-cultural people. Because of a shortage of government aid funds, my wife agreed to let me give them $5,000 of our savings (a large amount at the time) via the Vietnamese Province Chief to help them. The tribe was not informed of this; it was to appear that it was government money and resources.

These people had no numbers in their language; they were mostly spirit worshipers, had a very strict social order, did not steal nor lie. To be with these people in wartime in a hostile area, they who had suffered so much, not of their causing, to be my honorable friends, accepted as one of them. Well...it was difficult to top that.

Before I left Vietnam, M'bloi's village was invaded by North Vietnamese. The US Air Force napalmed it, reported no survivors. Why?

I had no knowledge of this note and letter from M'bloi until I opened my files from March 2006. They had been sealed since 1968.

M'BLOI - EBAN

— XIN CHÀO ÔNG WAGNER
Ở lại đây được mạnh giỏi, và
Tôi xin cảm ơn ông nhiều lắm, vì
ông đã giúp tôi trong thời gian mồ côi cha
ở tại đây/
— Một ngày gần đây chúng ta sẽ
gặp lại thì thật đầy đức —
Kw/60/62

```
         FROM: M'Bloi Eban

     Goodbye Mr. Wagner.

         I wish you a good health. And I don't forget
     to thank you for your help during my stay here.

         I expect I should see you later.

                              October 17, 1967
                              S/ M'Bloi Eban
```

-à-
Camarade
- Mr. HARRY. D-WAGNER, CHEF/CORAS/CH/SCTZ

- Avant de quitter votre maison, je vous remercie beaucoup, parce que vous m'avez aider beaucoup dans un mois.

- MA famille doit à vous remercié beaucoup et elle vous aime bien et considère comme un frère de leur maison.

- MA famille et moi ne vous oublient jamais et aujourd'hui le 19/10/67 nous quittons votre maison sans bonjour pour souvenir notre main droite.

- Je vous demande pardon, vous ne le pensez pas trop, ce n'est une mauvaise conduite et ne n'êtes timide pas comme les femmes portant le ventre.

Bientôt nous-nous rencontrerons dans un beau jour à Quảng-Trị (QRG-NQHTG)

- Je remarque et rappele tous les jours et tous les heures dans mon cœur.

- Enterminent, je vous remercie et avec un grand respect et je vous salué verticalement avec la main droite -,-

le HA-TRANG, le 19/10/6
votre Camarade

[signature]

19. Glộ. 58 ur

A LETTER FOR THANKS

TO : Mr. Harry D. Wagner
Chief, CORDS/CH/2CTZ

    Before leaving your living Quarters, I feel a deep thanks toward your strong help during my stay here.

    My family owe you very much. We consider you as a brother of ours in our own house.

    We think we always owe you and never forget you. And today we return home without saying farwell to you. It's no good at all.

    Please excuse me, dear friend. Don't be angry with us. It's not a bad conduct at all, you know.

    We hope we will see you later in Quang-Duc in a nice day.

    We always think about the days and hours when we stay in your house.

    Finally, we feel deep gratitude toward you and we respect you a great deal. I should geet you with my right hand, dear friend.

    Nhatrang, October 17,67.

    S/M'Bloi Eban

FORTY FUNERALS

I AM RELUCTANT TO WRITE ABOUT THIS BECAUSE I WAS SO VERY MUCH OFFENDED BY THIS POLICY.

    In our interrogations of POWs and Chieu Hoi, we repeatedly got the indication that the North Vietnamese were not reporting the loss of any troops sent to the war in the South.

After a tremendous battle between an American Division and a North Vietnamese Division in Kontum Province, both sides had heavy casualties, and afterward, there were up to 200 enemy dead on the field of battle. When I arrived after the battle there were three Buddhist monks on the field; exactly why I did not know, but I took pictures of them.

From a Psychological Operations perspective, maybe we should inform the North that they are losing persons in the South; made sense to me. This particular Division was tough and honored themselves in combat; they actually won the respect of the Americans.

We hatched up a plan. I had the Chieu Hoi trade shop make 40 wooden funeral boxes, got 40 parachutes off flares, and had my art and printing shop make up a document with the picture of the monks honoring a grave. With my connections with the Air Force, they agreed to drop these over Hanoi. The mission was to go in one week with everything all set.

I got a call from the J-1 at Region II IFFV of the General Staff to report as soon as possible. I knew and liked this officer, Col John ------ as a friend. I reported in. He said, "This is a direct order, a direct order from the highest authority of government. Stop your Hanoi operation."

He said it was a *national policy* not to register Oriental graves because they were considered subhuman. At first, I thought this was a joke, but he enforced his order by saying, "I advise you in all seriousness *do not to violate this order.*"

Well, I stopped it.

The Chieu Hoi wood shop sold the boxes to Vietnamese relatives of victims probably murdered by the Phoenix Program.

I am sure this was not the intent of any American I have ever met, but probably some higher Pentagon General who suffered as a prisoner of Japan. This is a strange world. (We lost 58,000 Americans in a country we considered the population as subhuman.)

Men working in the Chieu Hoi wood shop.

GIVE ME YOUR PRISONER

It all started up in the central highlands, where I crossed paths with a CIA member trying to get a prisoner being held by an ARVN Division of an NVA Colonel recently captured. The CIA was trying to intercept high-value enemy officers before the ARVN turned them over to the American military for interrogation. The CIA thought they had better methods than army intelligence.

I said, "Give me a name, and I will see what I can do for you."

I went into the Commander's office and asked for the man, and in five minutes, after a day of trying by the CIA, I said, "Here he is, all yours."

It didn't take but a week, and they (CIA) asked me to get another one for them. Before I left Vietnam, I had obtained eight NVA senior officers for the CIA before they were processed by the official channel to the American Army. There was apparently a dispute between CIA and General McChristian of MACV intelligence.

This was one of those "Get Wagner" circumstances. I assume the ARVN knew me or of me, and they would cooperate only with me. The CIA would contact me, send an Air America plane (C45 small 2 engine) for me, and we would go to the nearest airstrip. I would go get the prisoner, and we would fly back to Saigon.

Some of these flights were very long because we were active in all of South Vietnam. Normally the Air America had just a pilot, but these flights had a co-pilot. I was taking flying lessons from the right seat on the usual flights, so I asked why the co-pilot; the answer was this was considered a very high priority flight It was good to know that the NVA officer was of more value to my government than me (just something to keep in mind before you volunteer for anything).

I never had any trouble with the North Vietnam officers; they were not tied or restricted when I picked them up. I introduced myself, shook hands, and motioned for him to follow me to the plane. A couple of times the flight crew was not too happy with it. They, the prisoners, did not speak English, and I did not speak enough Vietnamese to carry on a conversation. I would show them pictures of my family, wife and four small children; this usually started sign language and relaxed the prisoner, got some smiles from them. You never know what cooperation and understanding can do for you.

I THOUGHT SHE WAS DEAD AND BETTY CROCKER

I was in Saigon on my motor scooter, on the street about four blocks from the center of the city where an enemy rocket had hit in the middle of a city block and pretty near burned it down. Along the street sidewalk, there was a body wrapped in plastic unattended; I stopped to see what this was about and recognized that of a young bar girl I had seen in a bar and grill a couple of blocks away. She was alive but had a high temperature and had excessive coin marks on her. Coining was a traditional medical procedure that consisted of filing a coin until it was sharp and then using it to make cuts along the body.

An older lady came up and said she was the girl's aunt; they lost everything in the fire two nights ago. The girl had been there on the street since the fire. I told her to get a cab and took them to my hotel, the Regina, and arranged for the hotel to get medicine and to feed and look after her for a few days until I came back in town. I spent 95% of my time out of Saigon, and the Embassy assigned me an apartment. I got the girl's life story and found that her family ran the auto repair shop for most of Vietnam south of Saigon. I gave the aunt a key to my apartment and told her to stay until the girl got well and they found a place to live; I would be out of town for two weeks.

On my return, they cooked a big dinner for me, so I baked a batch of brownies that they took home with them. Next day the aunt wanted to know what that was; she took them to work with her, and the children of her employer wanted more. It turned out the employer was the owner of the Saigon Central Market. He maintained strict neutrality about the war. His villa was surrounded by a high red brick wall with closed gates. Few, if any, visitors had been inside, especially not Americans.

I gave her a box of Betty Crocker Brownie mix and explained how to bake them. Two days later she asked me to go to work with her; they wanted to meet me. So, I went over and met the family for a few minutes and left because I understood his need for neutrality. On leaving, two Americans approached me, identified as CIA; it seemed they kept the residence under 24-hour surveillance. They wanted to know who I was and how and why I got inside. I gave them a simple answer, Betty Crocker. I doubt if they ever figured it out.

The young girl's information and ability to travel anywhere without question made her a most valuable source of observation and intelligence; her information unquestionably beneficial. She made some very dangerous intrusions into Viet Cong locations for me. I never told anyone about her, for the security of her and her family. The Viet Cong frequently traveled by bus and truck and frequented her family's garage. Intelligence is where you find it and recognize it. (The brownies at the commissary).

This is the young girl with her aunt.

INTIMIDATION (THE DARK SIDE OF CIVILIZED WAR)

It is with great hesitation that I display this subject; it is one that upsets me and brings anger as to why it is allowed within the American military.

We were in the field looking for hamlets, to expose them to the Chieu Hoi Program because all these hamlets and villages have had members impressed into the VC. We came into a hamlet of 12 or 15 houses, and from their looks had been well built and showed age. It was an established grouping with gar-dens and well-worn trails. What we found... I still have a clear mental picture of the 26 bodies we found dead; they had been shot down by American military.

It looked like five or six families were killed, but the one that has left its mark was the young, beautiful 25-year-old or so mother holding a baby in her arms when both were killed. We searched for other villagers but never found any. Other hamlets had not heard of the killings or seen any one of the villag-ers. We could not isolate which American unit was responsible, but my remedy for whoever did this was certain.

This was mostly an isolated case, but there were too many incidents of this lack of control of troops. When you hear some bragging about this type of conduct...we as Americans are better than this.

Now on the other side, the intimidation of villagers by the VC was even uglier.

In a village of 30 or more families, there was a young village chief who refused to support the local VC battalion with food and shelter. He and his family were staked out for punishment as a message to the village. The chief and his wife were tied to a fence and both their forearms were compound fractured and made useless; then their six children, age 2 to 12, were clubbed to death in front of them. Then the parents were eviscerated while still alive. The VC ordered that the bodies must not be moved for two days as a lesson.

To enforce cooperation from villagers, family members were taken; children were cut with the loss of a hand or foot as a warning for their parents. This was a death sentence from infection and the mother, to stop the pain, would smother her child as the only viable option. I carried morphine syringes with me so that would not be necessary.

Not all VC did these things; mostly they were in provinces where there had always been a criminal element that had then attached itself to the VC. I called them "thugs." I think from reports that the US Military has allowed too many deaths and has awarded members for body counts as a measure of combat success.

MY FIVE VIETNAMESE TEACHERS, NOW ONLY FOUR

I have been told I never show emotion; that's not true. My living quarters in Nha Trang was a rented two-story house on a busy street. There was a flight of stairs to the second floor that set close to the street sidewalk. Every morning that I was there, I sat on the steps to put on my shoes and socks and had a cup of coffee. On 100 of those days, five little preschoolers from the Buddha school a block up the street would pass by, and they could never understand the socks. I spoke very little Vietnamese, and they had no English; so, we began to exchange languages, and they would demonstrate the songs they had learned in school. Now, all of these kids looked like the typical Vietnamese, a page boy hairstyle, white blouse, and a full pleated skirt, blue and white that would flare out with just a little twist. The first lesson was shoes and socks; the second was "Itsy bitsy spider" with finger motions and flared skirts. Those mornings with the five lined up performing made life worth living in Vietnam. One of the five lived next door and always had a smile and greeting.

One day when I was out in the field a US Army jeep rounded the corner and struck my little friend. She was decapitated in front of her home. As an American, I could not pay my respects in this situation. The day after her bur-ial the Buddha school received a thousand-dollar anonymous gift, and I did visit the family to pay my respects after 90 days had passed. I had tears the whole visit. I had never felt so helpless before.

Special Forces put up a sign at that corner:

SPEED LIMIT 15 MPH

STRICTLY ENFORCED

COMDR GENERAL IFFV

You hardly get used to the war deaths in the field, but my five-year-old friend was not in the war. I remember every one of those 100 days and still tear up thinking about it.

MY FRIEND THE PROVINCE JAILER

My neighbor in Nha Trang was the Chief Jailer and a man of good character and reputation with contacts all over Vietnam. His family, wife, five children ages 4 to 16, and a mother- in- law, were all very orderly and family orientated, an attractive family.

Although I tried to remain obscure, I had a reputation in US military circles of influence with the Vietnamese. Fair enough, because most of my work was with the Vietnamese and since I was not enthralled with the American career enhancement concept of claiming all credit for themselves, and not giving credit to the Vietnamese who earned it.

Well, one day an American General, two stars, showed up by himself unescorted at the office, a little surprising, to say the least, unusual. "Well, General what can I help you with?"

"My girlfriend has been arrested and in jail." "Where?", I ask.

"In Saigon, two days ago."

"Why?"

"Extortion."

"How did you find me?"

"One of the officers in the Intelligence Section at MACV gave me your name."

"What is the young lady's full name?"

I wrote down the information and reassured the General. "Well, I don't know, let me see, come back 10 AM tomorrow. Do you have a place to sleep tonight?"

"Yes," he answered.

Of course, I got her out with no money; my influence and friendship with my neighbor paid off. All told, in the next six months, I got 14 ladies out of various jails, all for senior American Military officers. I never asked anyone's name, but I got more cooperation out of Saigon Headquarters MACV than you could believe any time I asked.

In Chieu Hoi we spent time with the military units in the field to promote the Defector Program. A few times with a brigade you would have thought I was the second coming for the good treatment. I often wondered what this General's girlfriend could have looked like.

While in Manila, I did get the jailer a TV, a better model than available in Vietnam PX.

On return trips to Nha Trang, I always stopped by his house to see the family. Friendship, fairness, and respect pay off sometimes in strange ways.

MY NEIGHBORS BECOME UPSET

I would say for Vietnam my living quarters in Nha Trang would be lower middle class, a mix of residential and commercial.

I had brought the Mnong Chief to Nha Trang for training, and he was to bring his wife and son; well, he showed up with a much younger second wife. My upstairs had a kitchen, bath, two bedrooms and large dining-living room; downstairs was office, one bedroom with a makeshift bath, and the house-keeper's room and bath. I usually lived upstairs because the lower floor bed-room was windowless and sandbag lined like a bunker. The plan was for the Chief and wife to occupy the upstairs, and I was to sleep in the bunker. This was to be for 45 days.

The van arrived with Chief, wife, son, and younger wife, and I took them upstairs to show them around; now they had never lived in a house, used a bathroom or a kitchen. It took all of my Latin and the Chief's French with much pointing and gesturing to get them settled in. Meantime, there was a lot of noise outside. I was confronted by 25 Vietnamese neighbors, all housewives. What the hell did I do now? I knew all these ladies; we were on good friendly terms. Finally, someone told me what the action was all about. They all decided it was totally wrong for me to live with the younger wife; they were protesting that. Well, we had three languages and no interpreter to settle things down. So, I invited all of them in for a tour of the house. I showed them that all my clothes were in the downstairs and to get upstairs you had to use the outside stairs. The ladies left nodding their heads ok.

Well, then the two wives started saying "frizzy, frizzy." We finally figured out they wanted a permanent hairstyle. So, I gave them money and pointed them in the right direction. Two hours later they returned all smiles, with Afro hairstyle sticking out 18" over their heads and attracting a lot of attention from the local Vietnamese, pointing and laughing. So, I picked the ladies up, one under each arm, with all three fully clothed. into the shower, and we shampooed most of the "frizzy" out. The neighbor lady showed up with brush and ribbons and fixed my two star borders up with a better hairstyle. Educat-ing the Chief and his family was quite an experience and an education of their cultural heritage for me.

I would have stood between them and a bullet any time; money and education do not necessarily make good, strong character. Character is how you deal with life.

There was a very sad ending to the Chief and his tribe; a year later the American Air Force napalmed his village, no survivors.

REFRIGERATOR AND FOUR BRICKS OF RAW OPIUM

I was in Saigon on my scooter and stopped at the new Military NCO billet back of the Rex Hotel in the center of the city just to try out their new Mess (restaurant). As I entered a couple of sergeants recognized me, and we got into a conversation. Chieu Hoi and Nha Trang came up, and another Master Sergeant approached, "Are you the one?"

"One what?"

"The weekly activity reports."

"Yes, so what?" I replied.

"I want to talk to you," the Master Sergeant said.

We found a table, and he explained that he worked at MACV in the report rewriting section where all field reports were edited before being sent to Washington. He began by telling me, "We can't edit or cut and paste your report."

"I know," I replied. "We heard about your group changing the reports, so we decided we wanted our work unedited."

The Master Sergeant respected that.

He proceeded, "Do you know where we can get a refrigerator? They won't give us one for the new billet."

"Meet me here Thursday, 11 AM with a truck."

To make the story short, I didn't really steal it; they just don't know who signed for it.

I now had for one refrigerator access to the central data center of MACV, which my security clearances allowed my access. I was accessing unedited report data that none of my superiors even knew existed. This gave us hamlet and village profiles necessary for our field operations. This was invaluable in setting up our field operations tests.

Two young (25-28) civilian men came to join us at the table; DEA agents. I did not know why they were in Vietnam. They were looking for drug smugglers, but in four months had not found any. So, I told them to mark a copy of the Armed Forces newspaper so they could identify it. "Order me a cheese-burger with fries; I will be back in five minutes," I told them.

I returned with a Polaroid of me holding four blocks of raw opium and holding the newspaper. I never told where I got it because I had agents in the same area. The Chinese (Cholon) did not cause me or the war any problems; it was their business, not mine. The Vietnamese knew of the location; a cop took the picture.

Take advantage of what you see and hear; keep alert for associations and information, always, everywhere. Always protect your sources.

REQUEST FOR ISSUE OR TURN IN (AR 735-28)	ISSUE ☐ TURN IN ☐	SHEET 1	NO. OF SHEETS 1	REQUEST NUMBER		
1. FROM: Mr. HARRY WAGNER	6. DATE MATERIEL REQUIRED		7. PRIORITY			
2. TO: SGM E. ROTH, RM #25, PHOENIX BEQ	8. VOUCHER NUMBER		POSTED	DATE	BY	
				DATE	BY	
3. ACCOUNTING AND FUNDING DATA	a. COST ACCOUNT CODE		b. WORK ORDER NUMBER			
4. FED STK ITEM IDENTIFICATION	c. NAME AND MANUFACTURER GENERAL ELECTRIC	e. MODEL	f. SERIAL NUMBER	d. POPULATION		
a	STOCK NUMBER, DESCRIPTION, AND CODING OF MATERIEL AND/OR SERVICES b	U/I c	QUANTITY d	SUPPLY ACTION e	UNIT PRICE f	TOTAL COST g
1	GE REFRIGERATOR SERIAL # 00955; 6Cu Ft, AID # 11.282 & #68-12816 (Received from USAID Wharehouse on 18 Mar 68 with fragment hole on top of box)	1	1	1		
////////////LAST ITEM///						
☐ FUNDED ☐ UNFUNDED ☐ CONSUMABLE ☐ NON-CONSUMABLE ☐ CREDITABLE ☐ NON-CREDITABLE					SHEET TOTAL	
ISSUE—I-Initial, R-Replacement	TURN-IN—U-Unserviceable	S-Serviceable			GRAND TOTAL	
Q. ISSUE OR TURN IN OF QUANTITIES IN "QUANTITY" COLUMN IS REQUESTED	DATE 5Jul68	BY SGM HARDT, J.W.	11. RECEIVED QUANTITIES IN "SUPPLY ACTION" COLUMN	DATE 5Jul68	BY	

DA FORM 3122, 1 APR 66   REPLACES DD FORM 1150 (for Army use) SUPPLIES OF WHICH WILL BE USED UNTIL EXHAUSTED.   1

RIFLES FOR THE UNITED STATES AIR FORCE IN THAILAND

One day in 1967 two Americans came into my office in Nha Trang and asked if I could help them; they were sent to see me. Well their problem, they were supposed to interrogate Chieu Hoi and POWs for information of bomb damage in North Vietnam. It seemed the Army would not cooperate with the Air Force to collect this data. So General Cherry of CINPAC sent these two Majors to get this information. The Army had not provided any help for two months, and they had been totally ignored.

They could not use Air America or gain entry to POW compounds or Chieu Hoi Centers. We had a problem; I asked them to get orders from their General assigning them to me at Chieu Hoi. In two days, they were back with the orders, which I forwarded to my CORDS superior. I got them priority flight status countrywide for Air America, wrote orders for the Vietnamese to grant access passes for all POW and Chieu Hoi compounds and to provide all assistance requested. They came back after three weeks to thank me, and their commander thanked me. Thailand had a request if I could help locate 36 car-bine rifles from those with serial numbers captured by Chinese in the Korean War.

What? They said there are such rifles and could I help. I checked with Colonel Ladd at Special Forces and it is possible; so, we put the word out and we got 36 carbines with serial numbers as captured weapons. They looked in bad shape but operable; next day a plane from the Thailand Air Base arrived at Nha Trang to pick up the weapons. The following day we received a message of thanks and all of the numbers checked.

I asked the Majors what the rifles were for. They had created an indigenous force to go further off base to patrol for invaders, and they did not want the force to be identified as American.

You never know how far friendship and cooperation will take you.

Director, OCO Region II
Mr. Robert L. Patterson

May 3, 1967

Harry D. Wagner
Assistant Director for Chieu Hoi
OCO Region II
Exploitation of Hoi Chanh for USAF.

    To expedite the collection of Air Force intelligence for the 6499th collection group, Hawaii, whose primary source of data are the Hoi Chanh and POW's, I have taken their II Corps group under my OPCON in order to coordinate their efforts with the other agencies working in the Chieu Hoi Program.

    They have agreed to service other requirements which I might levy on their team which would promote the exploitation of intelligence from their interrogations. Their interrogation and interpreter abilities will help alleviate one of our biggest field problems.

    They have expressed that their recent efforts through my coordination and contacts have made their successes possible. And that other Corps Areas have been unable to assist them to the degree that OCO in Region II has in their assigned mission.

RECOMMENDATION:

    A Memo be sent to OCO Prov Reps and Chieu Hoi Advisors to assist where and when possible the following agents:

                  Jim Harrier
                    Ben Vachon
                    Le Truong Xuan

SMALL WORLD

    I was in central Vietnam on the Cambodian border working psy-ops and was scheduled to be the Tet house guest of the Vietnamese family who owned the best restaurant in Nha Trang. I caught a US Air Force flight into Saigon; the airfield was under attack. I was warned of an attack at Tet and had all of my people in safe locations two days earlier. My plan was to clean up and get an early flight to Nha Trang. I got my scooter and made it into the Regina hotel by 8 PM and received news of how large an outbreak, country-wide, had started. We could see the VC mortars firing from the cemetery and heard a lot of rifle fire. Then the helicopters came to shoot up the VC in the cemetery.

At daylight, the Embassy called me to come in; this is an eight-block walk, and no one to be seen anywhere. I arrived at the Embassy, only a few rifle rounds popping off, but the MPs formed a protective box around me, and we all ran for the Embassy door (which showed considerable damage). We opened the door and got inside safely. I went up to the 5th floor, the CIA area with only two people in the building, the radio room men. They said for me to sit here and answer this phone.

I could hear reports coming into the radio room; this was a very serious happening.

The phone rang so I answered; "American Embassy, Saigon Can I help you?"

"This is Rostow. Why hasn't the press got word of the 35,000-enemy dead?"

I replied, "Sir, I don't think we know. I will get someone for you. Hold on." I later left the Embassy and went back to the hotel where they were organizing to go out to secure some of the people who were in the areas still with fighting.

Sure enough, two days later, "Wagner, go confirm the enemy dead count."

Well, I put enemy dead first two weeks at 17,000, non-combatants (civilians) at 13,000. This did not include at that time Hue or Danang.

The Marine who opened the Embassy door lives in Madison, Georgia, the same small town I live in. It is a small world.

THE 27 PRISONERS OF WAR

Somehow the Chieu Hoi Compound we built super-sized in Binh Dinh received 27 young VC female militants from another region further north. They were, when captured, armed with AK 47s, as a well-organized combat unit. There was no place to put them, so they sent them down to us. They were not defectors but POW. The first time I came across them in the compound they were all in one dorm and had not come out for meals, which were therefore taken to them. If 27 pairs of eyes could kill, I would be dead. They cut me into a thousand pieces; as the compound commander was telling me the story, I made no indication that I was concerned about the ladies.

A week later on another visit the same reaction, but I had brought a couple dozen combs and placed them on the window sill and walked away. I had noticed on my first visit they had tried to make a comb out of scrap wires. Vietnamese women kept their hair in Vietnamese tradition very long.

After the third week, they were still staying in the dorm. This visit I left six bars of French soap and some hair brushes, and again I made no recognition of them. When I was in the compound I ate the food and lined up with inhabitants.

The fourth week I left shampoo and ribbons and still made no recognition of them. The compound had several training programs, woodworking, tailor, hair cutting, shoe repair. These women were age 16 to 25, under five feet tall, slender, generally nice-looking people. There were two in the tailor shop, but the rest stayed in the dorm and still took meals there. My next trip, same routine but with two bolts of cloth, not black.

The next visit was two weeks later, and I got there just in time for the meal. So, I was standing in line, and I heard this giggle behind me. That's right; 27 POW's looking good, all smiling at me. Later we heard their life stories of how they were impressed into the VC to protect their family members from intimidation by the VC. They gave us no tactical intelligence, but we did learn how to touch the minds of the population in our favor.

These ladies could field strip an AK 47 quicker and reassemble it faster than anybody I have ever seen. Small but tough, foot speed super-fast, they could really move...strong...I would have adopted every one of them.

Some of the 27 POW in the dorm at the Chieu Hoi facility.

An experience that brings a memory with a smile; an appreciation and love of the Vietnamese. They learned about an American who was there by choice, not in a uniform.

THE DRAGON LADY

A Sweep, like a Search and Destroy to pick up enemy in an area considered secure produced about 30 possible enemy.

Most were local people, friendly or supportive of the Viet Cong and were being held in a temporary holding compound, which was nothing more than a fence with no facilities to hold suspects for the interrogation teams to work through them. All was apparently routine until they approached the Dragon Lady. This woman, typical Vietnamese in appearance, but she had a real mean vindictive streak. She would have none of it and attacked her interrogator, spitting and scratching. Thus, the label "Dragon Lady."

Now I had developed my own approach to such problems.

On the third day, conditions were getting pretty bad in the compound, and most of the interrogation was over. They had allowed the inmates to set up a chair for haircuts under a poncho so as to give them something to do. I won't rate the other interrogators, but I carried eye ointment, antibiotic oint-ment, peroxide, and waterproof bandages to treat the minor cuts and bruises because the compound was getting a little dirty and minor abrasions were getting infected. So, I am the First Aid man, no questions asked, just some assistance offered. I noticed the Dragon Lady near the haircut tent and the chair empty, so I went over, sat down and asked for a haircut. They used a comb and straight razor. You would have thought she saw a ghost. She cut my hair, pretty good job, so I tipped her 20P, thanked her and left the compound. She was an active VC officer and never gave up any information. She trans-ferred to a POW compound to serve out a 15-year term. I found her a month later and brought her a letter from her family. I provided her paper and pen to write to her family; she was a strong, proud woman convinced her actions were right. The world needs more like her.

She wrote her letter, which I delivered. She also wrote the names and locations of VC officers from a different command than hers. I later had her transferred to the Chieu Hoi Program.

It was a big score, the capture of the senior command of a whole brigade size VC group. The Dragon Lady wanted to be shown respect; that's all. Civility is never out of place; it always works for you, not against you.

THE FOUR MILLION

In my capacity of controlling Psychological Operations for IFFV, it required me to approve all leaflet drops as to the content of the leaflet text. The mili-tary units must submit copies through my office for approval to have the leaf-lets printed; I controlled the presses. I returned from the field after three days to review requests; I rejected one for reason of being a blatant threat of in-timidation. The leaflet had a drawing of a soldier holding a rifle over a Viet-namese family group with the wording of "you must tell us where the Viet Cong are or we will bomb your village." I rejected the leaflet, and then the storm began.

Unknown to me at the time, the leaflet was the work of a Division Commander, a Lt General who had pushed it through the printing operation without my approval. When my psy-ops company got word it was rejected the SHTF; here they come. We have on orders of the Division Commanding General printed four million leaflets to be dropped over the total area of his command. I said *destroy them*. I held the rank as a General on the IFFV Corp General Staff.

Now I have the General in a very bad mood at having his brilliant psy-ops plan canceled. I told him no; it had been rejected. *Destroy the leaflets*; this would be a boxcar stack of paper. Off he went to the IFFV Commanding General who said *destroy the leaflets*. He was still not going to be denied his plan, so he went to Commanding General MACV; *destroy the leaflets*.

The psy-ops military personnel was generally considered second-rate by the line company (combat) personnel. So, word of this escapade spread and created its own legend as a boost for psy-ops. A Division Commander got stood down by psy-ops personnel; I think the lesson here is wrong is wrong. Even a General can't influence the decision with his Academy connections, but he kept at it; it even got all the way up to the White House. *Burn the leaflets*.

I spent less than three minutes in this and made a decision. After the fury had died down we went up to the General's location and worked out a program for his division. I think he was a good commander and had an outstanding record of accomplishments in Vietnam. He underestimated my authority in supporting psy-ops operations in Vietnam.

The story ends with a General with a wounded ego and a great boost for the importance of Psychological Operations.

In my case in hindsight, I think it was more detrimental for me to display this much authority and not be a part of a personnel power group.

It took three months, 24/7 to *burn the leaflets*.

THE MIDNIGHT FLIGHT

With the impact of the Tet attack and until MACV could get reports in from all their deployed units, the military grounded all aircraft. No helicopters were flying for two days. Apparently, there were some military-CIA outposts run-ning out of supplies by the second day and needed to be resupplied before the air cover would resume.

As far as I know, two Air America helicopters were going to fly the second night of Tet after dark to deliver supplies to several of the outposts. The Air America craft has no guns or armor plate. We were loaded with 15 cases of ammunition and two drums of gasoline and medical supplies.

They had two flight crews volunteer to fly the very risky flights but needed someone to push the cargo out on delivery. Since everything was closed down they had few choices, so I went with one of the two crews for two flights. I knew the Air America crews were the best, and I also knew what would happen to the outpost if not resupplied.

I was into my second day without sleep and don't remember much about the airtime except it was uncomfortable on the long ride trying to sleep on top of two drums of gasoline. We were flying with no lights and on a compass heading; the crew was in contact with the outpost, and it had been attacked repeatedly and was out of supplies.

The flight crew said they were to approach the outpost above 10,000 feet; the outpost would blink their lights once, and we would align to a touch down position. He said he would drop straight, stop two feet off the ground and I had 15 seconds to unload. Oh my God, now they tell me, and on departure prepare for serious evasion maneuvers. I understood, unloaded out of both sides and just as I felt lift-up a man appeared, and I handed him the medical supplies, which included whole blood.

The second flight was about the same, how the aircrew could stop the downward descent I do not know. It felt like we were at terminal velocity, free falling. I checked the next day, and military relief got to those outposts. The two flights, it seems, violated a general order restricting all flights, but the CIA and Special Forces weren't about to lose four outposts.

What a night, the second night of Tet. We got back to Saigon at 4:30 AM, and I got called back to the Embassy. They sent me out to report on the progress of the Vietnamese police who were in a house to house fight with a large VC-NVA force in Saigon, less than a mile from the Embassy. I had Vietnamese Special Police Branch ID and could get through their perimeter checkpoints.

I reported back that the Vietnamese police were pushing the fight and the VC were getting hit hard. The bombing by the Vietnamese Air Force was gen-erating thousands of refugees leaving the combat area, and they were creat-ing a lot of confusion.

My next assignment, do something about it...

MAKING A WAY FOR THE REFUGEES

The next project I was assigned was to expediate the flow of the Vietnam-ese refugees trying to escape the bombing by the Vietnamese Air Force. Thousands of people were trying to escape by means of one road and it was getting bogged down. These people, who were day laborers, unloaded cargo from the ships docked in the harbor. They had been living in temporary shelters, some as little as a cardboard box and plastic. The Tet attack forced them to leave even these improvised shelters. I was also told the White House wanted to know the condition of the refugees forced out of the harbor area of Saigon due to the Tet attack. They had seen the turmoil of the thousands of people fleeing the area.

As I approached the area I could see that the flow of people was being blocked by a truck parked on the bridge. There was no other way to escape but to cross that bridge, so I went to investigate. The truck was parked across, so there was little room to get around it. An American missionary was there; he was handing out religious literature and pamphlets. I politely told him he had to move; he was blocking the way and the refugees were not able to get out fast enough. He refused to leave his post until all the literature had been passed out. I then told him that people were getting killed because of this delay. At his second refusal, I had to direct him at gunpoint to move his truck; he complied.

The message from the White House was that from what they saw on TV, the refugees did not appear to have their personal belongings with them. I observed hundreds of people go past me. I was able to explain to the Embassy officials that the Vietnamese possessed very little. Their most valuable possessions were a metal cook pot, straw sleeping mat, and three or four pieces of silk clothing which would fit in a package about the size of a pack of cigarettes.

On my way back out, I saw that the bridge was blocked once again by the same truck. This time I did not ask politely or ask at gunpoint. I went to the truck, put it in gear and pushed it into the harbor. The literature that he was so determined to distribute to the Vietnamese, which was causing people to not escape bombing and gunfire, was all written in English. I never saw that man again.

THE NVA MAJOR AND THE GENERAL

I am not sure I know all there is to know about NVA Major Tan; he was processed as a defector to the South Vietnamese Chieu Hoi Program. My view is different from the South Vietnamese information, and my data, I am sure, is more the true story. He was a North Vietnamese Major from Lang Son, a northern province on the border with China as a Deputy Province Administra-tor. He had been in the South for most of four years. He was very intelligent, spoke Vietnamese, Chinese, and French fluently, very socially mannered. I assume he was part of the shadow VC government as an administrator and not as a fighter.

The US, CIA, and ARVN held and questioned him for a month, determined he had no tactical data of any importance.

I found him walking along a road in full NVA uniform and stopped to give him a lift and find out who he was and where he came from. I took him back to Nha Trang and put him up in my living quarters and made him part of my Chieu Hoi staff. He was full of small bits of information, like the nearly four years he had been in the South he had not sat in a chair or ate from a table. His descriptions of conditions of the VC were very practical but limited; many from the North never had the opportunity to see the freedom and the pros-perity the South had. We began to use some of this in our psychological approach to gain defectors.

Well, it was a slow day so I took the Major in my jeep over to the IFFV Headquarters. We drove it right through security, and he was dressed in his full NVA uniform. I can accept that the guards knew me well enough. I took him to the Commanding General's office. We walked in, "General Rosson, I don't think you have had the opportunity to meet the enemy up close. This is Major Tan of the North Vietnamese Army." I had no idea what would happen.

The General spoke French, and he and the Major spent most of an hour in conversation; seems the General was in Vietnam after WWII as an observer to the French. I had left them alone and had other business in Headquarters. When I returned the two were standing, and the General shook hands with the Major and thanked me for the opportunity and the visit.

This wasn't the last time the General and I had to solve a few problems dealing with the Vietnamese. The General's name, Rosson, one of the few outstanding officers to serve in Vietnam.

My association with General Rosson was very good, actually with the creation of the unified command, CORDS, I was made a General in the new organization on his General Staff. This helped my fieldwork and kept my interaction with the military very cooperative. My staff assignments were control of all Psychological Operations and second seat for Military Intelligence for IFFV, Region II.

Major Tan, former North Vietnamese Officer.

THE PALM READER

One of the most remote provinces in South Vietnam centered at Gia Nghia on the Cambodian border. It is the land of Mnong Montagnards (you will find them mentioned in other places in this book).

The Vietnamese Province Chief's fiancée was the Saigon inter-military social palm reader and fortune teller. One trip there the young lady wanted to read my palm; so, I obliged. I, on afterthought, should have not. It seems my left palm had this very unusual lifeline indicating an everlasting life; in other words, I will not die again. That is, according to her. Well, the word spread fast among her friends in the upper crust of Vietnamese society. All this was unknown to me.

Gia Nghia is not much more than crossroads in the jungle, land of tigers, elephants, and rhinos, but an interesting place to spend a little time away from everybody. One night there the little village got overrun by a VC battalion and the Province Chief called for me to come to his house. I arrived, and we went driving in his jeep, two bodyguards in the back. I was in front with him. It was my thought we would go out to the MACV sector for safety or further out to the ARVN artillery firebase.

No such luck, he headed straight into the village market square where 60 VC were holding the villagers for a political lecturer. There was only one road in and out of the square; here I was in this jeep circling the square where I could have hi-fived all 60 VC. I asked him what the hell was he doing; he looked happy. Well, he wasn't finished. He went past the 20 VC guarding the main road; they actually had to move out of his way. He, with a big yell, finally headed home. He was convinced since he was with me, he would not be harmed. I never wanted to be in a vehicle with him again. A month later I was at the MACV Compound, and he showed up. I learned we all were going about 25 miles up country via road to shoot crocodiles in a lake. He wanted to try my S&W 357 six-shooter. In the past, I always made this trip by helicopter. After an hour on the road, it turned into a trail, and we came across burned out trucks and tanks; this road had not been traveled since the French left. Here we were, two jeeps in enemy territory, an hour or better from help. The Chief said, "We have Wagner; we are ok." My visits became few and far apart.

Until the Tiger hunt.

My lifeline palm got me into a Vietnamese society and their families that the Embassy had been unable to do and gave me contacts otherwise unknown to the American Mission. It gave me introductions to the top Vietnamese government officials and military.

THE TIGER HUNT

I was in a helicopter traveling from Pleiku to Quang Duc to observe a tiger hunt as a guest of the Province Chief of Quang Duc Province. The tigers were large and could take 150-200 pounds in their mouth and run off as though it were nothing. The VN was losing people; they did not like the tigers. We were about ten minutes away from the Province when we got an emergency radio call to go to Tuyen Duc where a FAC pilot was shot down. We were the closest chopper and would be first on the scene. We made a landing near the crash site; a gunner and I went to the small plane. The pilot (American) and his spot-ter (Vietnamese) were both dead. We removed their bodies from the crash site and loaded them into the chopper. Then further communication came in informing us that it was a VN engineering battalion that was being ambushed. It had seven American enlisted men with it. So, I started to cover the convoy while it was being attacked with small arm fire. I began searching for the Americans, as well as any Vietnamese, who were still alive. None were found alive, American or Vietnamese.

We began to load the Americans in the chopper; when loaded we waited for assistance. The air cover had arrived and was circling overhead, and two choppers (gunships) came in. We left for the Province headquarters to unload. We arrived in Quang Duc just as a chopper was taking off. It was going up, and about 5,000 feet the main rotor stopped and it crashed. I missed the flight by three minutes.

Losses that day:
- Crew of copter   2
- Gunners   2
- Province Chief   1
- Province Chief bodyguards   2
- USAID (Advisor and Deputy)   2
- MACV sector officers   2

Eleven men lost that day, all were great guys and good friends.

Lest We Forget Vietnam

United States	58,119	Killed
	153,303	Wounded
	1,948	Missing
South Vietnam	230,000	Killed
	1,161,763	Wounded
North Vietnam	1,100,000	Killed
	Unknown	Missing
Vietnam	4,000,00	Civilians Killed

CHAPTER 9

CREDENTIALS

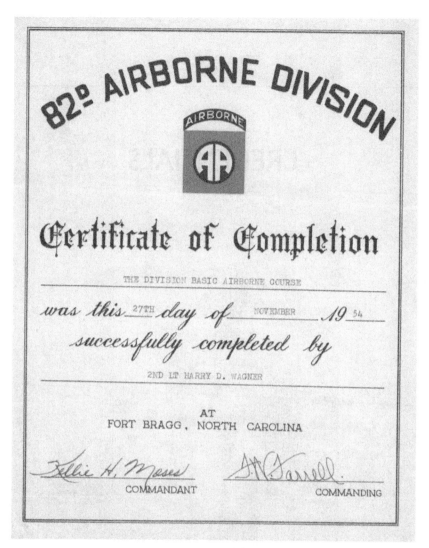

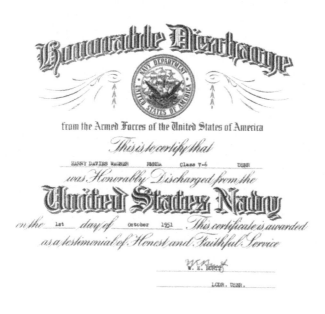

1.	26 F 0430 6815 wagne 010866 082866 fSO farl 1867 1 2 082866 022769 082866
1. NAME (CAPS) LAST-FIRST-MIDDLE	WAGNER, HARRY D. MR.
3. BIRTH DATE	06-26-30
4. SOCIAL SECURITY NO.	297-26-7271
5. VETERAN PREFERENCE	1 — NO
6. TENURE GROUP	A/FE
7. SERVICE COMP. DATE	11-03-64 (4)
9. FEGLI	1 — COVERED
10. RETIREMENT	1 — CS
12. NATURE OF ACTION	171 EXCEPTED APPOINTMENT — FOREIGN SERVICE RESERVE LIMITED CODE NTE 02-27-69
13. EFFECTIVE DATE	08-28-66
14. CIVIL SERVICE OR OTHER LEGAL AUTHORITY	SEC 625 (a) (2) FOREIGN ASST ACT OF 1961, AS AMENDED
20. TO: POSITION TITLE AND NUMBER	PROVINCIAL REPRESENTATIVE #1717-99
21. PAY PLAN AND OCCUPATION CODE	FR-0340
22. GRADE OR LEVEL	(03/03)
23. SALARY	pa $16941
24. NAME AND LOCATION OF EMPLOYING OFFICE	US A.I.D. TO REPUBLIC OF THE PHILIPPINES MANILA, PHILIPPINES
25. DUTY STATION	SAIGON, VIETNAM
26. LOCATION CODE	95-7000-945
27. APPROPRIATION	72-1171006; 756-50-430-00-69-71
28. POSITION OCCUPIED	2 — EXCEPTED SERVICE
29. APPORTIONED POSITION	42 STATE TEXAS

SUBJECT TO SATISFACTORY CLEARANCE ON THE BASIS OF LOYALTY, SECURITY, AND SUITABILITY INVESTIGATION.

WAITING PERIOD FOR STEP INCREASE BEGINS WITH EFFECTIVE DATE OF THIS APPOINTMENT.

THE APPOINTEE HAS RECEIVED A COPY OF M.O. 443.1 – EMPLOYEE RESPONSIBILITIES AND CONDUCT.

EMPLOYEE HAS THE OPTION ON THIS ASSIGNMENT TO (1) HAVE HIS DEPENDENTS RESIDE IN THE UNITED STATES AND SERVE AN 18 MONTH TOUR IN VIETNAM; OR (2) WITH APPROVAL OF AID/W HAVE HIS DEPENDENTS TRAVEL AT GOVERNMENT EXPENSE TO AN OVERSEAS LOCATION AND SERVE A 24 MONTH TOUR; TRAVEL OF DEPENDENTS TO BE PERFORMED UNDER PROVISIONS OF M.O. 560.2.

31. DATE OF APPOINTMENT AFFIDAVIT: August 29, 1966

34. SIGNATURE AND TITLE: M. S. BARBITTA, CHIEF ADMINISTRATIVE, EMPLOYMENT BRANCH

32. OFFICE MAINTAINING PERSONNEL FOLDER: OFFICE OF PERSONNEL ADMINISTRATION, WASHINGTON, D.C. 20523 — FE BUREAU

33. CODE EMPLOYING DEPARTMENT OR AGENCY: ST-02 AGENCY FOR INTERNATIONAL DEVELOPMENT

35. DATE: 07-28-66 msh

1. EMPLOYEE COPY

HEADQUARTERS 82D AIRBORNE DIVISION
Fort Bragg, North Carolina

SPECIAL ORDERS
NUMBER 174   EXTRACT   21 July 1955

35. 2D LT HARRY D WAGNER 04002542 Armor 44th Tk Bn is placed TDY w/Armd Sch Ft Knox Ky to attend Armd Commo Crs (17-O-7). WP rept comdt NLT 27 Jul 55. Upon completion (o/a 20 Oct 55 unless sooner rel) will rtn proper sta. Tvl by common carrier. TFA auth but not directed. Fiscal copies of all expenditure documents will incl citation of BVN AQ-323. TCS. TDN. 2162020 653-4002 P2271-02-03 S31-001. JTR will apply. Vou claiming reimb for auth tvl expenses will be submitted within ten (10) days after completion of tvl. Off has been cleared for access to classified info & mat to incl CONFIDENTIAL. Auth: TWX Hq 3A AJTNG-7-296 dtd 22 Jul 55.

BY COMMAND OF MAJOR GENERAL TRAPNELL:

OFFICIAL: KENNETH E. ECKLAND
                                         Colonel, GS
Walter H Pierce   Chief of Staff
WALTER H. PIERCE
1st Lt, AGC
Asst Adj Gen

DISTRIBUTION:
   "S"

N-153
9/67

USAID / VIETNAM

NOTIFICATION OF CHANGE OF DUTY POST OR POSITION ASSIGNMENT

NAME: Wagner, Harry D.
GRADE: FSR-03
EFFEC DATE: November 30, 1967
Country Code: 0733

FROM:
Title: RED Dev Adv Reg
Psn. Grade: FSR-03
Psn. No: C 0592
Seq. No: 0405 (old number)
Duty Post
 Corps, Province, District, City, Saigon: II CTZ HQ, Nha Trang
 Organizational Location
 Office / Division / Branch: CORDS/Chieu Hoi Div

TO:
Country Code: 0731
Title: Prog Insp. Off
Psn. Grade: FSR-02
Psn. No: 2PAA
Seq. No: 0050
Duty Post
 Corps, Province, District, City, Saigon: Saigon
 Organizational Location
 Office / Division: CORDS/Phoenix Div (formerly ICEX)

PERMANENT ☐   TDY ☐   DAYS

Prepared by: JL Lovess
Date: 3/19/68

Approved: Myna B. Wheat, Deputy Chief/CORDS/PER
Date: 3/19/68

INSTRUCTIONS:

USAID Personnel Officer prepares form on employees assigned to USAID/Vietnam who are being reassigned to another position within USAID or, with CORDS concurrence, to CORDS headquarters or to the field (CORDS Regions). CORDS Personnel prepares form on employees assigned to CORDS headquarters who are being reassigned to a new position either in CORDS headquarters or in the field, or with USAID concurrence, to USAID headquarters. CORDS Regional Offices prepare form on employees assigned to the region who, with CORDS headquarters approval, being reassigned to a new position and/or duty post in the field. CORDS headquarters forward to USAID Personnel Officer.

DISTRIBUTION: AID / W / Data Control / Personnel File / ADFM / Locator Record / C&R / CORDS Headquarters Regions.

AID 4-98A (11-87)

VIET-NAM (Short Form) PERFORMANCE EVALUATION REPORT
Foreign Service Reserve Officers
Foreign Service Staff Officers and Employees
DEPARTMENT OF STATE
AGENCY FOR INTERNATIONAL DEVELOPMENT

CHECK ONE BOX
☐ REGULAR REPORT
☐ INTERIM REPORT
☒ DEPARTURE OF RATED OFFIC
☐ DEPARTURE OF RATING OFFIC
☐ CHANGE OF DUTY

Name of Officer Being Rated (Last, First, Middle): WAGNER, Harry D.
Officer's Class: FSRL 03
Classification Title of Position: Program Implementation Officer

Date of Birth: 06-26-30
Post or Organizational Symbol: Vietnam
Officer's Functional or Organizational Title (if any): Psychological Operations Advisor

Date of Arrival at Post: 09-26-66
Period Covered by Report: December 1, 1967 to August 9, 1968

Rating Officer Signature: [signed] William Law   Date: 7 Aug 68
Typed Name: William Law
Typed Class, Title: GS-14, Ch, Ops PHOENIX Staff

Reviewing Officer Signature: [signed]   Date:
Typed Name: Evan J. Parker, Jr.
Typed Class, Title: GS-16, Director, PHOENIX Staff

I have received a copy of this report from my supervisor.
Signature of Rated Officer: [signed] Harry D. Wagner   Date:

GENERAL INSTRUCTIONS TO RATING OFFICERS
1. Read official instructions on performance evaluation before completing form (See Manual Order 423.2)
2. Prepare in triplicate – Original for Washington, Copy for post, Copy for employee.
3. Evaluate the Officer on the basis of the difficulty and importance of the duties he was required to perform.

PART I – DESCRIPTION OF MAJOR DUTIES AND RESPONSIBILITIES
(List in descending order of importance the major duties and responsibilities assigned to the Rated Officer.)

Item	
1.	Psychological Operations Advisor to Director, PHOENIX.
2.	Develops doctrine promoting PsyOps in a classified program for specialized objectives.
3.	Draws up procedures to implement above.
4.	Devises specific operations.
5.	Devises evaluation procedures.
6.	Promotes appreciation for PsyOps through frequent field contacts both with US and GVN.

Number and Types of Employees Supervised:
-None-

REVIEW PANEL
A. Was review panel used? ☐ Yes ☒ No
B. Panel's comments. Use additional sheets if necessary.

Members: Name _____ Title _____ Class _____

Signed: _____ for the Review Panel.   Date: _____

PROFESSIONAL EVALUATION PREPARED FOR HARRY WAGNER

OBJECTIVES: A position emphasizing public relations, marketing and sales management responsibilities or a position as sales representative in industrial/technical sales. An ideal position for Mr. Wagner would be one which combined customer contact and sales functions with managerial and adminsitrative duties. One in which he would neither be tied to a desk or travel extensively.

Mr. Wagner wants to explore possibilities outside of his present porduct area, machine tools. He has no prefrences regarding specific products, but would be well-suited for a wide range of technical and engineering products which might include machinery equipment and the like. He is especially interested in exploring "growth industries", such as environmental control and municipal technology. He would also be interested in a consulting organization, along the lines of the Rand Corp. (but not the Rand Corp.).

SUMMARY: "Mr. Wagner has a broad and diverse vocational background which includes industrial and mechanical engineering, marketing and sales, and public administration. In the consultant's opinion he is ideally suited for a managerial position related to sales, marketing and public relations in a technological area.

Mr. Wagner is a very bright man who possesses a mind which is imaginative, creative, and flexable, as well as analytical, logical and precise. He has excellent human relations skills and comes across as an engaging and involved person. He appears to have good skills for using other people effectively and for supervisory work, for assessing, selecting and motivating others. Also, he impresses as a person who should excel in planning, organizing and coordinating work. Mr. Wagner appears to be one of those individuals who have the capacity to deal very effectively and equally well with both complex problems of a technological nature, and human relations problems, one who can bring to bear his technical mind on a variety of organizational and marketing problems.

In the terms of personal style Mr. Wagner is an assertive, competitive and tenacious man who is energetic, determined and ambitious. He is a self-assured person with a solid perspective on himself and his life who behaves in a confident, decisive manner and who seems quite mature emotionally. He impresses as a person well able to function in positions of authority, in making decisions and determining policy and taking calculated risks.

In conclusion, Mr. Wagner demonstrates well developed strengths in areas of management and administration, human relations and marketing, and excellent potential for further growth in these areas. He should excel in technical sales, customer contact and public realtions work, in creating, planning and organizing relative to the full range of marketing functions, and in general management, supervision and administration. In the consultant's opinion he would be an excellent candidate for an upper level position emcompassing the above functions."

February 1971

J. FREDERICK MARCY & ASSOCIATES, INC.

CHAPTER 10

PHOTOS

The following pages are pictures that I took while I was in Vietnam. They are not photos of the war damages or the loss of Vietnamese civilians. I respect the lives of the Vietnamese as equal to those of Americans; they are not "subhuman" as I was told.

I am standing with a view of Binh Dinh Province to the west.

Open street markets in Vietnam.

Cao Dai Temple, located in the province capitol of Tay Nihn, near Cambodia.

Dalat Palace, an exclusive hotel built in 1922. I stayed there whenever possible.

My third week in Vietnam, I crossed the demilitarized zone (DMZ) and entered North Vietnam. The Province Chief of Quang Tri told me he had a weekly chess game with a Province Chief in North Vietnam. He told me where I could cross, using a board over a large gap in the bridge over the river. The Polish military guard waved as we entered the DMZ.

A nationally recognized choral group sponsored by the South Vietnamese government. I helped them with transportation country-wide after learning of their problems getting through war-torn areas.

HARRY WAGNER — THE HEADLESS SNAKE

This is the Vietnam I want to remember.

EPILOGUE

Following my refusal to assassinate a Vietnamese family for the Phoenix Program, I was unceremoniously asked to leave Vietnam in September 1968. I had written an official request to transfer out of Phoenix and back to USAID. I was called into Colby's office and he told me he wanted me out of the country in two days; normally it was two weeks. In the short time it took me to return to my apartment, I found that CIA agents had already packed up all of my belongings, personal and official. Everything was prepared to be shipped to the United States. This was most definitely a mistake on their part and is the reason why I have all of my original and classified documentation. Even though guns were not supposed to be shipped, the CIA packed my personal 12-gauge shotgun, .308 rifle, and three .30 caliber revolvers.

I flew to Manila and prepared my family to leave. My wife had already begun her second-year teaching English at the American School but had to leave her position and her students behind. She was a much loved and respected teacher. She and our children barely had time to pack, much less say goodbye to friends and coworkers they had met while living in Manila.

To Ma'am, with Love

The easily broken heart of the A.S. Indian was shattered once more. Squanto had to bid a sad farewell to one of the most beloved missionaries ever to set foot in the jungles of the A.S. campus. She departed via a mechanical eagle on August 10.

Mrs. Harry D. Wagner came to the A.S. for the 1967-1968 school year to teach English. She left, having taught much more than the difference between an elegy and an eulogy, that Melville did not eat blubber, and that Jack Frost was not, in any way, related to one Robert.

Her departure has imbedded a sense of great loss in those of the seniors who were lucky enough to have had Mrs. Wagner for English III. She brought life into what one expects to be a course in dullness. A rapport was created between teacher and student that bridged the wide crevice of suspicion and mistrust, until it was hard to distinguish any difference of levels.

Who can forget the delightful tales of her hamsters? And the simple joy of hearing her give a pinch by bite account of her children fighting? The guitar lessons in the midst of the showdown of the Grangefords? Finally, how about dropping in at her house in Magallanes, on Margarita Street (you could drop in at any time because she was always glad to see you), and seeing her on the floor strumming her guitar in the middle of her children and those crazy hamsters?

If this sounds more Lycidic than front-pagey, it is with good reason. To those of us who were blessed with her acquaintance, this is a period of mourning. How the juniors last year were hoping that she would teach English IV! And what a disappointment it was to know that this year's juniors had all the luck.

Mrs. Harry D. Wagner attended Miami University and Ohio State. She received her B.S. in Education in the former; she was honored with an additional award at the A.S. This is not a tangible award; no cups; no placques; no ribbons. This is the only award that counts. She won our Hearts.

Mrs. Harry D. Wagner, B.S. Ed., M.A. in Happiness, Ph.D. in Warmth. Mrs. Wagner — a teacher.

Upon arrival in the United States, as I was still employed by the State Department, I attended a conference to promote and recruit new personnel into USAID. During this time, while in Washington, D.C., I ran into Jonathan Ladd, Commanding Officer of Special Forces, Detachment. He was surprised to see me back from Vietnam. After learning of my situation, he invited me to work with General Westmoreland in his new group prepping upcoming military in foreign engagements at the Pentagon. I politely declined; my experience in Vietnam was more than enough military in my lifetime.

I stayed active politically and was a staff member of the Nixon election committee in South Carolina. For the next 50 years, I worked and had a successful career, only stopping to care for my wife after a devastating cancer diagnosis. I raised my family and retired in 2007. When I moved and unpacked my attic, I found boxes full of material from my office in Vietnam. These were items I had not looked at since 1968. Reading and following the reports that were coming out of our country's involvement in Syria, the careless civilian deaths and the destruction of Damascus, I noticed an eerie parallel to my time in Vietnam. After reading through my reports from Vietnam, I began to pore over information on the current activity of our military and our government. This book began as a newspaper editorial. What I continued to find was disheartening and alarming.

My hope for you, the reader, and the rest of my country is simple; peace. I have stated my critiques, but more importantly my plans for our government reformation and military transition. I am not foolish enough to think this will happen quickly, but every day of change is a day closer to the realization of peace and pride for our country, here and abroad.

In closing, I would like to quote two famous Americans, one well known for his military leadership in battle, and one for his homespun, practical sense humor. Both leave us with words of wisdom for a changing world.

"People grow old only by deserting their ideals. Years may wrinkle the skin, but to give up interest wrinkles the soul. You are as young as your faith, as old as your doubt; as young as your self-confidence, as old as your fear; as young as your hope, as old as your despair. In the central place of every heart there is a recording chamber; so long as it receives messages of beauty, hope, cheer and courage, so long are you young. When your heart is covered with the snows of pessimism and the ice of cynicism, then and then only are you grown old; and then, indeed, as the ballad says, you just fade away." -General Douglas McArthur

"In the beginning of a change the patriot is a scarce man, and brave, and hated and scorned. When his cause succeeds, the timid join him, for then it costs nothing to be a patriot."
-Mark Twain

Peace Team Forward

Hòa bình Đội ngũ Chuyển tiếp

Team de Paz Adelante

Equipo de Paz Adelante

Peace

GLOSSARY OF ACRONYMS AND ABBREVIATIONS

AFSAM an electro-mechanical rotor-based off-line cipher machine
APA American Psychological Association
APT Armed Propaganda Team
ARVN Army of the Republic of Vietnam
CG Commanding General
CIA Central Intelligence Agency
CINPAC US Commander in Chief Pacific
COIN counterinsurgency
COMUSMACV Commander, US Military Assistance Command, Vietnam
CORDS Civil Operations and Rural Support
DOD Department of Defense
EIT enhanced interrogation techniques
FSRO Foreign Service Reserve Officer
GCHQ Government Communication Headquarters
GVN Government of (South) Vietnam
HDQ headquarters
HSOC Human Science Operation Cell
HTT Human Terrain Team
HUMINT human intelligence
ICEX Intelligence Collection and Exchange
IFFV I Field Force, Vietnam
JSOC Joint Special Operations Command
MAAG Military Assistance Advisory Group
MACV Military Assistance Command, Vietnam
MOS military occupational specialty
MSM main stream media
NCO'S noncommissioned officers
NONCOMS noncommissioned officers
NSA National Security Association
NVA North Vietnamese Army
OCS Officers Candidate School
PICS Provincial Interrogation Centers

PKSOI	Peace Keeping and Stability Operations Institute
PLA	People's Liberation Army
PRC	People's Republic of China
PSY-OPS	psychological operations
RIF	reduction in force
ROK	Republic of Korea
SOCOM	Special Operations Command
SP-OPS	Special Operations
UCMJ	Uniform Code of Military Justice
USAID	United States Agency for International Development
VC	Viet Cong